"In *Helping Your Anxious Child*, parents are provided a step-by-step guide for assisting their children in overcoming a panoply of worries, fears, and anxieties. The strategies described are well-established ones, backed by considerable scientific support. Parents will find this book engaging, easy to read, and full of important ideas about how to best help their children."

> —Thomas H. Ollendick, Ph.D., University
> Distinguished Professor in the department
> of psychology, Virginia Tech

"Written with hope, optimism, and respect for children's feelings and unique differences, this book is an important new resource for both parents and professionals working with children. The authors clearly describe, explain, and demonstrate how to help children build the necessary courage and self-confidence needed to face troublesome fears and worries. This excellent reference will make a difference in the lives of many children who struggle with the pain of anxiety and worry."

> —Debra Whiting Alexander, Ph.D., author of
> *Children Changed by Trauma*

"Parents want to help their anxious children but often do not know how. Here at long last is a book designed just for that. It offers extensive and concrete steps to teach the child to cope with anxiety, using the means of behavior and thought. This book is highly recommended."

> —Elke Zuercher-White, Ph.D., author of
> *An End to Panic*

Helping Your Anxious Child

— SECOND EDITION —

A Step-by-Step Guide for Parents

RONALD M. RAPEE, PH.D.
ANN WIGNALL, D.PSYCH.
SUSAN H. SPENCE, PH.D.
VANESSA COBHAM, PH.D.
HEIDI LYNEHAM, PH.D.

Publisher's Note

Distributed in Canada by Raincoast Books

New Harbinger Publications, Inc.
5674 Shattuck Avenue
Oakland, CA 94609
www.newharbinger.com

Acquired by Tesilya Hanauer; Cover design by Amy Shoup;
Edited by Elisabeth Beller

Library of Congress Cataloging-in-Publication Data

Rapee, Ronald M.
 Helping your anxious child : a step-by-step guide for
parents / Ronald M. Rapee .. [et al.]. -- 2nd ed.
      p. cm.
 Includes bibliographical references.
 ISBN-13: 978-1-57224-575-4 (pbk. : alk. paper)
 ISBN-10: 1-57224-575-1 (pbk. : alk. paper)
1. Anxiety in children--Popular works. 2. Anxiety in
children--Treatment--Popular works. I. Title.
 RJ506.A58R37 2008
 618.92'8522--dc22

2008039779

FSC
www.fsc.org
MIX
Paper from
responsible sources
FSC® C011935

16 15 14

16 15 14 13 12

To my "girls"—Wendy, Alice, and Lucy
—Ron Rapee

To Loyis and John
—Ann Wignall

To my family and friends
—Sue Spence

To Tom, Will, Alex, and Gabriella
—Vanessa Cobham

To Andrew and Emily
—Heidi Lyneham

Contents

Acknowledgments

The anxiety management principles and program described in this book are based on the clinical treatment program, *Cool Kids*, developed at Macquarie University, Sydney, Australia. *Cool Kids* is an evolving program that is based on many years of scientific research, theory, and clinical feedback. These developments could not have come without the invaluable input from a countless number of researchers and practitioners. It is simply not possible to mention or thank all the many people who have influenced this program. However, special thanks for the most recent developments go to Maree Abbott, Jennie Hudson, Susan Kennedy, Carolyn Schniering, and Viviana Wuthrich. We would also like to acknowledge the pioneering work of Paula Barrett, Mark Dadds, and Phil Kendall.

Introduction

WELCOME

Being the parent of an anxious child can be a roller coaster. While anxious children are often thoughtful and caring, they can also be exasperating and place extra demands on parents in terms of time and emotion. Often extended family and friends do not see the distress being experienced by both the child and his or her immediate family. When a child always seems to be scared of something and begins to miss out on so many of life's rewards, most parents are desperate to help. So it is understandably frustrating when nothing you do seems to work. Sometimes the things you try seem to make children worse in the long term, and because most people think that children will "just grow out of it" at some point, many families suffer for a long time before they find out that something can be done.

Anxiety is a common problem among children and adults alike, and there are many successful treatment programs run by professionals that have been developed to provide much-needed help. The program you are about to embark on is different. It is an adaptation of the proven professional programs designed to allow parents to teach anxiety management skills to their own child.

This book is designed to guide parents through a structured course of readings and activities that will help you to teach your child to manage his or her anxiety and will help you to learn new ways of responding to anxious behavior. Each chapter includes children's activities, to encourage children to be actively involved in taking control of their anxiety, and practice tasks that will help you and your child to practice new skills in everyday life.

We hope that you enjoy the program and that your child conquers his or her fears and worries by successfully learning anxiety management skills.

HOW TO USE THIS PROGRAM

We know that every child is different and so is every family. So there are no hard-and-fast rules in running this program, and if you think of a better way to do something, then we encourage you to try it. But we have had many years of experience in running programs like this one and in working with children and their parents. Based on this experience, we can share with you some of the principles that work best for the majority of families.

First, the activities and readings in this book are best completed in the order they appear. Each set of readings and activities is designed to build on the last set. If you jump ahead, you may find that you haven't yet learned the previous skill and that will make progress much more difficult. Some children, however, will move more quickly or more slowly than others. So how fast you work through the chapters is up to you and should be based on your child's own personal circumstances. In the activities you will be encouraged to include several examples of the same task. If your child catches the idea of a particular activity after one or two examples, it is not necessary to complete the rest of the examples. If your child needs the extra practice to grasp the ideas, then complete all of the examples. For some children, you may need to spend two or three weeks on the same chapter and exercises and repeat them all. Don't be afraid to try again—it is much better for your child to be a little bit bored than to not understand.

You will need to set aside time in your schedule to work on the program if you want to see your child managing anxiety. We recommend that you make a particular set time each week to be your "anxiety management session." This does not mean that you only work on your child's anxiety at that time—far from it—but this will be the main time that you read over the next chapter, talk with your child about the tasks and activities, and plan the next week's exercises and practice. For example, you may decide that Sunday mornings after breakfast will be your anxiety management session time. Think of it like another season of dancing or football or piano. Every Sunday morning for a few months, you will sit down with your child to work on his or her anxiety management skills. You need to make sure this is possible. For example, plan your weekend activities around this time and make sure that the rest of your family are either part of the program or occupied somewhere else.

You will see three types of activities described in this book. First, in the main body of most chapters, you will find "Parent Activity" sections. Reading the chapter and doing the parent activities are tasks that *you* need to do *before* you sit down with your child, to prepare you for the anxiety management session. Most of the time these will be issues you need to think about or skills that you need to learn in order to help your child. Next, at the end of each chapter, you will find a set of "Children's Activity" sections. These are the activities, exercises, and lessons that you need to go over with your child so that he or she can learn to manage anxiety, and these should be done during your weekly anxiety management session. Each child activity has some notes for you, the parent. These notes provide a short, simple description of what you need to explain to your child (based on what you have read in the chapter) and an example of a completed worksheet that uses the anxiety management skill. Your child will need blank copies of the worksheets so he or she can practice the skills during the week. You can make your own blank worksheets by using the completed examples in this book to guide you. Alternatively, you can download the *Helping Your Anxious Child Workbook,* offered free to users of this book on the Internet at *www.ceh.mq.edu.au/hyac.html.* In the downloadable workbook, each activity described at the end of the chapters is available for use with your child and contains child-friendly explanations of the relevant skill for you to read with your child and blank worksheets (based on those used in the examples within the chapter) that your child can complete with your help. Finally, at the very end of most chapters, you will find "Children's Practice Task" sections. These practice tasks are the most important component. They describe exercises that your child will have to practice many times throughout the week in order to really learn the particular skill. These are the skills that your child will need to learn to manage anxiety, and so these practice tasks will need to be done many times, sometimes for several weeks, until your child gets really good at the particular skill. Worksheets for these tasks are also included in the downloadable workbook. The workbook is designed to save you time and to help you translate what you read into child-friendly language. It is, however, very easy to create your own worksheets by copying the examples provided in this book if you do not have access to the Internet.

A Few Things to Keep in Mind

The readings and activities should be completed over two to four months. Although it may be tempting to move through the entire program in the first week when you are feeling enthusiastic, it is better to work through it at a consistent pace. That way you won't burn out before the program finishes, and it will help to create the habit of tackling anxious thoughts, feelings, and behaviors on an everyday basis.

The program will work better if both parents work through the readings and activities. One of the most important features of a successful program is being able to put the skills into practice in all parts of the child's life, and this is much more likely if both parents know what to do. The same goes for any other adult who your child spends a significant amount of time with such as step-parents, grandparents, or nannies. If some of the anxiety occurs at school, then it might be helpful to meet with your child's teacher and talk about what you are trying to achieve. But if some of the people in your child's life are not interested in what you are doing, don't give up. We have seen some spectacular successes, even in cases where one parent had no interest whatsoever in helping with the program. The program is also very successful in single-parent families.

Finally, don't get discouraged by slow progress and setbacks. Keep in mind that your child has had many years to develop anxious ways of behaving and thinking; it will take more than a few weeks as well as a lot of persistence to change these patterns. Especially at times when you or your child are stressed—don't give up; find an enjoyable activity to do and then, when things are a little calmer, come back and keep on working.

Seeing a Mental Health Professional

We mentioned earlier that this book is designed to provide parents with all the information they need to help their child overcome anxiety. That's true. But we all know that knowing something and doing it properly are two different things. That is why we strongly recommend that you see a qualified mental health professional about your child's anxiety if you possibly can. If you picked up this book from a bookstore or through the Internet and you have not seen a professional about your child, this is particularly important. A mental health professional will be able to properly assess your child and let you know whether this program is appropriate for him or her. A professional can also help you to apply the information in this book to the specific circumstances of your and your child's lives. And a professional can help to keep you motivated at times when nothing seems to be working, or can help you adapt the program to get over those tough hurdles.

But if a professional gave you this book or told you to get it, then we are pretty confident it will help. Our scientific research with children who had been diagnosed with an anxiety disorder tells us that when parents were given a copy of this program and told to help their own child, with no extra professional help, around one in five children were completely free of an anxiety diagnosis after going through the program, and many more made strong gains. When several short sessions with a therapist were added to help parents stay on the right track, over 60 percent of children who completed the program were diagnosis free.

WHAT TO EXPECT DURING THIS PROGRAM

- *Don't* expect that you'll have things sorted out in just a few weeks.

- *Do* expect that there will be noticeable changes before completing the program.

- *Do* expect to make progress in a zigzag fashion rather than a straight line, that is, two steps forward and one step back.

- *Do* expect that any narrow, or highly defined, worries (e.g., where the only worry is being afraid of dogs or going to sleep in the dark) will be easier to make progress on than broad, or generalized, worries (e.g., getting worried about *any* new situation or social event that comes up).

- *Do* expect that children will need to keep practicing skills for some time after the program has finished, until their new skills in thinking and behaving are everyday habits.

Will Anxiety Go Away Completely?

Someone who has no anxiety at all would be in a lot of trouble! Anxiety is a normal emotion that helps us to perform to the best of our abilities and protects us in dangerous situations. The aim of this program is to bring anxiety down to manageable levels. We want children to manage anxiety so that they get the helpful effects, like revving up before a big game, without the bad effects, like avoiding situations that might otherwise be fun. As you will learn later, anxiety is also part of a person's makeup or personality. This program will teach your child new ways of coping so that anxiety should no longer rule his or her life. But you will find that even after finishing the program, your child will probably always be a slightly more emotional or sensitive person than some other children you know, and that is not a bad thing.

PARENT ACTIVITY: GETTING READY FOR THE PROGRAM

Here are a few summary points to think about to get you ready to run this program with your child:

- You will need to put time and effort into helping your child learn to manage anxiety, just like you would if you were helping your child learn the piano or to improve his or her reading.

- Your child will also need to have the time to put into this program.

- It will also be much better (but not absolutely necessary) if other important people in your child's life are also willing to help.

- You should plan a time that you and your child will set aside each week to complete an anxiety management session (around thirty to sixty minutes). You will need to make sure that the time is "reserved" and doesn't get pushed aside and that other members of your family have something to do and won't disturb you.

- You will need to be prepared to spend additional time outside of this session in practicing skills and repeating key points.

- As the parent, you will also need to set a time each week, before the anxiety management session, to read over the next chapter, do any parent activities, and be prepared for the session with your child.

CHAPTER 1

Understanding Anxiety

Emily had a secret problem. She was twelve years old and still afraid of the dark. At night, when her family was asleep, she would often hear strange noises outside and she would panic, imagining that they were being robbed or that they'd all be murdered while they slept. Emily still kept a night light on in her room and would often run to her parents' room on particularly bad nights and slip into their bed. She'd never take the garbage out at night or go upstairs alone after dark, and she usually insisted on her parents checking her room before she went to sleep. Because of her fear, which was a secret to everyone except her parents, Emily never accepted invitations to sleep over at friends' houses and found excuses to not go to summer camp. Emily's parents had tried to push her to face her fears and sleep in the dark, but she became so upset and they had so many fights that eventually they just gave in to her fears. Now her parents feel frustrated at the limitations that Emily's fear causes both in her own life and for everyone else in their family.

Ten-year-old Connor had a different problem. He was extremely shy. At home he would talk freely with his family. At school or with strangers, Connor was different. He was terrified that he would do the wrong thing and make a fool of himself. He hated to speak in front of the class. Even though he could play the piano beautifully, he was too scared to perform at the school concert. In the school yard he was usually alone, afraid to join in with the other children.

Problems like Emily's and Connor's are common, normal, and quite easily handled. But they can often cause unpleasant and potentially serious interference in children's lives and in the lives of their families. Their stories give you a quick look at some of the many different ways that anxiety can affect children's lives.

Fear, worry, and anxiety in children can take many forms. All children experience fears and phobias at particular stages of their lives, and this is a normal part of growing up. For example, we know that young infants will develop a fear of separating from their mothers at the same time they begin to fear strangers and new people. A little later, most children will be scared of the dark, and at some point, many young children begin to imagine monsters under the bed and burglars at the door. In the teenage years, self-consciousness and shyness become a very common and often annoying part of developing maturity. When these fears develop, they're usually just part of the normal developmental process that we all go through. But sometimes, fears and worrying can reach a point where they start to cause a problem for the child. These excessive fears are often temporary and transient but may still cause such distress that as a parent, you want to help your child hurry through this stage. On the other hand, some children will experience fears and worries to a much greater degree than their peers, and some continue to experience fears long after other children their age have outgrown them.

Some fears can be very understandable and based on obvious causes. For example, children may be scared to go to school because they are being bullied; or they may be scared of the dark following a burglary at home. In other cases, the fears and worries that children experience are much harder for parents to understand. For example, the child who worries that he or she is stupid may be doing perfectly well at school and elsewhere in life. Or a child may be scared that Mom will be killed in a car accident even though Mom always makes sure she picks him or her up on time. Or a child may worry about and imagine every possible disaster even though nothing really bad has ever happened to him or her. In these cases the anxiety may be an entrenched part of the child's personality, and you may feel as though your child has been sensitive and "high-strung" for all of his or her life.

Many adults believe that childhood is a time of carefree days and no responsibility. It may surprise you to know that in fact, anxiety is the most common problem reported by children of all ages. Diagnosable anxiety disorders are found in around one in ten children, and less extreme but still distressing fears are even more common. Anxiety and worry affect children of all ages, from infants to adolescents. Girls or boys, rich or poor, brilliant or average—it makes no difference—anxiety can affect anyone. Some parents may think, "So what? Everyone gets nervous sometimes. It doesn't hurt anyone, so why all the fuss?" To some extent, these parents may be right. Anxiety is not as dramatic a problem as a child contemplating suicide or engaged in drug abuse. But anxiety is a sign of real personal suffering—it's not an act or a way of getting sympathy (although in a few cases this can complicate the picture). Anxiety can also cause marked interference in children's lives, bringing down their school performance, interfering with friendships, and affecting the whole family. In addition, in some cases, anxiety in childhood can be the beginning of a lifetime of anxiousness that, in severe cases, can lead to the more serious problems we just mentioned—drug and alcohol abuse, depression, and even suicide. If you're a parent with an anxious child, you need not fret or worry excessively—anxiety can be managed—but it's good to be motivated to do something to help your child.

Managing anxiousness and helping your child to develop confidence and control in life is much the same no matter what form the anxiety takes. In this book we will describe some of the common types of children's anxieties, increase your understanding of children's anxiety, and teach you how you can help your child master his or her fears. We will discuss all sorts of anxieties—from the minor, temporary fears that many children experience, to the longer, more severe, and invasive problems that can so extensively restrict a child's life. Most importantly, we will describe, in detail, skills and strategies that you can use to help your child to learn to control his or her fears.

We will begin our discussion of anxious children by describing several children who we've seen and who have benefited from these strategies. We'll come back to these children throughout the course of this book and use them to show how each of the techniques can be applied to the real world.

SOME REAL-LIFE ANXIOUS CHILDREN

Talia's Story

Talia is a typical nine-year-old with a big group of friends and a cheeky streak. She loves rock music, is a member of the school basketball team, and rarely worries about a thing. But Talia is scared of water. She learned to swim when she was five years old, but she's never enjoyed it and has always avoided deep water as much as possible. When her father takes her out beyond where she can stand, she begins to panic, clings tightly to him, and begs him to take her back. No one can figure out why Talia is afraid of the water—she has never had a bad experience there and has never known anyone who has drowned. Both of her brothers love swimming and surfing. Yet something about the water has always been frightening to Talia, and, try as she might, she just can't talk herself out of it. Now that Talia is getting older and starting to go to pool parties and the beach with friends, she is running out of excuses and her swimming phobia is beginning to become a problem.

Kurt's Story

Ten-year-old Kurt is a worrier. He worries about his schoolwork, he worries about his parents' health, and he worries that he will forget to feed his dog and she will starve. Kurt's parents no longer let him watch the evening news because he spends the next two days worrying about all the tragic stories he has seen. They also don't tell him about new things that he is going to have to do until the very last moment, because when they do, he pesters them mercilessly with his constant questions about what is going to happen. This interrogation also happens whenever Kurt has to do something unpleasant, such as take a test at school or go to the dentist. Kurt will ask his parents for information and reassurance hundreds of times.

Kurt also worries about germs. He's scared when he touches certain things that germs have gotten onto his hands and that he will get sick and die. He worries about infections and all sorts of illnesses. As a result of his worries, Kurt washes his hands again and again all day long. For example, after going to the bathroom, Kurt will scrub his hands for several minutes. He will also rush off to wash whenever he has touched something he thinks may be contaminated, such as door handles and seats where other people have been sitting. Kurt refuses to go to certain places, such as hospitals or the cafeteria at his school, because of the germs he thinks are there. He will sometimes get particular ideas about things that are contaminated that will then become taboo. For example, he went through a phase of avoiding the backyard because the dog had once thrown up there. Last week, Kurt caught the train with his mother and they sat opposite a man who sneezed several times. When he got home, Kurt raced straight to the shower and washed for forty-five minutes.

George's Story

Now that he's twelve years old, George's parents believe that he should be doing a lot of things by himself. But George has little self-confidence and worries a great deal about what other people think of him. He has always been a nervous, sensitive, and shy child and he grew up having very few friends. Since beginning middle school this year, George has retreated even more into his shell. It took him most of the year to make his first friend, Tony, who is also a bit of an outsider. In class, George's teachers report that he rarely says a word and that he becomes very upset if he is asked to answer a question or speak in front of the class. At home, George is quite talkative with his family but becomes quiet if anyone he doesn't know well comes over. George has very specific rules about what clothes he can and cannot wear, he will always get his parents to deal with sales clerks and cashiers, and he will never answer the telephone. Despite his parents' urging, George has never joined a club or team and spends most of his time at home alone, building models. From time to time, George talks about feeling lonely, and he has gone through a few periods of feeling quite down and miserable.

Lashi's Story

Lashi is a seven-year-old girl whose parents separated when she was five. Since the separation, Lashi has begun to worry a great deal about her mother. She is terrified that her mother will be killed in a car accident or by a burglar and that she will never see her again. Lashi cries whenever her mother leaves her, and she refuses to be left alone with a babysitter or even to sleep over at her grandmother's home. As a result, Lashi's mother has hardly been out since the separation. She is beginning to lose her friends and has no chance to meet other men. Sometimes Lashi is willing to stay overnight with her father, but she spends the whole time asking about her mother, and lately she hasn't been willing to stay with him at all. Lashi's parents still get on well despite the separation, and they agree that they need to work together to help Lashi overcome her worries. It is a real struggle every morning to get Lashi to go to school, and sometimes Lashi's mother gives in and takes a day off work to let her stay at home. Lashi also worries about burglars breaking into the house and is scared of the dark. Over the past few weeks, she has begun to sleep in her mother's bed, something her mother has allowed because it is just too much of a struggle to argue. Lashi's mother loves her daughter very much, but just lately she has really begun to get fed up with the limitations on her life and is starting to feel angry and resentful.

In addition to her main anxiety, Lashi also has a fear of injections, doctors, and hospitals. Most of the time, this is not a big problem, but occasionally, it makes it very difficult for Lashi to go to the doctor's for treatment and even to visit a sick friend. Having shots is the biggest problem—Lashi missed her last vaccination because she would not allow the nurse to give her an injection.

Jess's Story

Jess is eleven. Her parents are worried about how Jess will ever cope when she goes to high school given how much she worries about everything. Jess worries when her parents go out, worries about keeping her friends, about doing well enough at school, about events from the past and in the future, and about possible dangers. She always expects things to go wrong and does not like to go outside her comfortable routine. Jess even worries about how much she worries. She has a couple of close friends at school but fears that one day they will suddenly decide that they don't like her. She doesn't want to make new friends in case that ruins her current friendships. Jess is a very bright girl, and she produces flawless work almost all of the time, spending hours making sure that everything is absolutely correct, but Jess performs very badly during long tests mostly because she gets stuck on an early question trying to make it the perfect answer and then doesn't complete the rest of the questions.

Recently Jess has developed a very big fear of choking when she eats. This started after a bad case of tonsillitis. After that, she stopped eating certain foods such as hard fruits and many meats because she finds them difficult to swallow. All other foods have to be chewed for a long time before she can swallow them. She now has different dinners than her parents and sisters and has lost some weight. Her parents have tried to force her to eat, but Jess only panics and starts hitting people and throwing food across the room.

These children show just some of the ways that anxiety can affect a child's life. There are many types of anxiety and many ways that children can show its effects. In fact, the forms that children's worries can take are as varied as the number of children themselves. As you can see, fears do not always have to be "weird" or "crazy." Many normal and common types of concerns can become a problem for children if they interfere with something children want or need to do. Fears and worries can also clearly vary in their intensity and effects.

The good news is that problems such as these can be managed very well. In the rest of this book we will describe the skills needed, including thinking realistically, facing up to fears, and learning better social interaction. Each skill will be described in detail, examples and activities will be provided, and we will apply the concepts to the cases of children we've introduced. Finally, we will discuss the future, what you can do to help your child maintain his or her gains and what to do if problems reemerge. Throughout the program your child will not only be building his or her confidence, but will also be earning rewards and time with you and the rest of the family. In our experience, most children going through the program enjoy learning the skills even if at times they get a bit scared of what they may have to do or embarrassed about what they think and feel.

IS YOUR CHILD'S ANXIETY A PROBLEM?

Everyone feels anxious from time to time. For most people, anxiety doesn't really affect their day-to-day life. Understanding more about "normal" fears and worries, and the ways in which fears can affect a child, will help you to decide whether your child needs help.

Normal Fears

Fears are a normal and natural part of life. They are part of our evolution as a species and they emerge and develop at specific times in our lives. Fear of strangers and fear of separating from the main caregiver will typically show up in children at around six to nine months of age. Naturally, the exact age and the amount of fear will vary slightly from child to child, but all children will go through this stage and most fears will show up at similar times. As a child gets older, he or she will begin to show other natural fears. Fears of animals (e.g., dogs) and insects (e.g., spiders), fear of the water, fear of the dark, and fears of the supernatural (e.g., ghosts and monsters) often start to show up in young children in the toddler years and beyond. Around middle to late childhood, children begin to be more aware of other children and will begin to become self-conscious and develop a strong desire to fit in. These worries usually increase over the following years and peak in mid-adolescence, when how a teen looks and what the other kids think of him or her become the most important things in the world.

When Does Anxiety Become a Problem?

How do you decide if your child's fear is "abnormal"? Quite simply—you don't! There is no such thing as an "abnormal fear." All fears are normal—some are simply more intense or more extensive than others. Even fears that might at first appear strange, such as a fear of germs that causes a child to wash a lot, can simply be seen as normal fears that have become too extreme. After all, most people worry at least a little about germs—just ask yourself if you would eat dinner out of your dog's bowl! So children with anxiety problems can simply be thought of as having normal worries that have become extreme and more intrusive than the worries of other children.

A better way to think about these things is to consider whether your child's anxiety is a problem for him or her. Does it interfere with or cause difficulties for your child? These difficulties may be many and varied. For example, it may simply be that your child's fears cause him or her to be upset and distressed. Or they may stop your child from doing things that he or she likes or from making friends. Or it may be that worrying is affecting your child academically or on the playing field.

The bottom line is this: if your child's anxiety is adversely affecting his or her life, then he or she will benefit from learning about how to overcome it. In making the decision to work on these skills, you should remember that change will take dedication, hard work, and commitment. But it can also often be enjoyable. The activities are not in any way harmful or dangerous, and they usually reap many additional benefits such as improved self-esteem, confidence, and general happiness.

How Common Are Anxiety Problems?

As we mentioned in the introduction, so-called anxiety disorders are the most common type of psychological problem found in children and adolescents. Approximately one in ten children meets the criteria for what is technically called an anxiety disorder. The particular disorders vary somewhat with age. Fears of separating from caregivers is more common at the younger ages, while social fears are more common at older ages.

Interestingly, even though anxiety disorders are so common in the real world, they are not the most common problem in child mental health clinics. Mental health centers for children are much more likely to see children with aggressive behaviors, attentional difficulties, eating disorders, or suicidal tendencies. What seems to be happening is that even though anxiety is common in children, most parents do not think of taking their anxious child to a professional for help. This may be because parents believe that anxiety is simply a part of their child's personality and that there is nothing they can do about it. Or it may be because anxiety doesn't affect the parent or teacher as much as these other problems, so they don't realize how much the anxiety is affecting the child. In addition, in many areas mental health services for children are more prepared for, and used to dealing with, aggression problems than anxiety. As a result, parents often feel that they are making "mountains out of molehills" in worrying about their child and may be discouraged from seeking help.

How Does Anxiety Affect Children?

Overall, anxiety doesn't have as dramatic an impact on a child's life as problems like drug use or delinquency. But problems with anxiety can still affect a child's life to quite an extent.

Anxious children tend to have fewer friends than other children their age. Because many are shy, they have difficulties meeting new children and joining clubs and groups. For this reason, they often have a limited number of friends and they may not interact with their friends as much as others do. In turn, lack of friendships can have an important impact later in life, increasing loneliness and reducing the opportunity for peer support.

Anxiety can also affect a child's academic achievements. Many anxious children do very well at school because their conscientiousness and perfectionism make them try harder. But they may not be doing as well as they could. This is especially the case for those children who worry a great deal. We often find that these children delay homework and struggle with their lessons, not because they are incapable, but because their worry stops them from approaching the tasks confidently. Anxious children may also get less out of the class and the teacher because their anxiety stops them from making full use of the resources (e.g., they may not ask questions in class). In addition, many anxious children may do well in the classroom situation but fail when it comes to exams because their worry about failing stops them from being able to concentrate. In the longer run, research has shown that anxious children have more-restricted choices and opportunities in terms of careers. Many careers such as sales, media, or legal work may be out of the question for shy adolescents because of their worry about performing in front of others.

While many anxious children will change as they grow and mature and may well become confident, outgoing adults, some will develop into anxious adults. Anxiety disorders in adulthood can be a serious hindrance in life. Anxious adults are more likely to abuse drugs and alcohol, miss work or be unemployed, have illnesses and visit a variety of medical specialists, and be depressed and even suicidal. Depression is likely to start even earlier, usually during adolescence. We aren't trying to suggest that this will happen to your child. But even if the effects of anxiety for your child are at the mild end—perhaps a few missed opportunities—it would be better to do something now than to wait until more severe problems develop.

TYPES OF ANXIETY

Everyone is individual, and no two anxious children will behave exactly the same way. But there are some broad similarities that we can describe.

What Does Anxiety in Children Look Like?

When children experience anxiety, they are likely to notice it affecting them in three ways. First, anxiety is experienced in the *mental processes* or *thoughts* that they have. Anxious children will have thoughts that center around some type of danger or threat. For example, they may worry that they'll be hurt, that someone close to them may be hurt, or that they'll be laughed at. Second, anxiety is experienced *physically* in the body. When a child becomes anxious, his or her body becomes more "pumped up" or aroused. Researchers often refer to this as the *fight-or-flight response* because its purpose is to help protect people by preparing them to combat or escape potential danger. The fight-or-flight response includes changes such as rapid heart rate, increased breathing, sweating, and nausea. Therefore, when worried, anxious children may complain of stomachaches, headaches, vomiting, diarrhea, or tiredness. Third, and probably most importantly, anxiety affects children's *behavior*. When children are anxious, they may freeze, fidget, pace, cry, cling, and shake. In addition, anxiety usually involves some type of avoidance. This may be obvious avoidance (e.g., refusing to take the garbage out in the dark), or it might involve more subtle avoidance (e.g., helping all night with the music at a party so they don't have to talk to anyone).

The amount of anxiety will vary from child to child. Some children are afraid of simply one or two things. For example, a child may be generally confident and outgoing but simply be scared of going to sleep with the light out. At the other end of the spectrum, some children may be worried about many areas of life and may seem generally nervous or sensitive. For example, a child may worry about any new situation; be scared to meet new children; be afraid of dogs, spiders, and the dark; and worry about his or her parents going out at night.

There are also certain common anxiety patterns that we see time and again, and we will describe these in the following sections.

Specific Phobias

A child with a specific phobia is afraid of a particular situation or object and usually tries very hard to avoid contact with the thing that frightens him or her. Some common specific phobias include the dark, dogs, heights, spiders, storms, and injections. Talia, who we introduced earlier, has a specific water phobia.

Separation Anxiety

Separation anxiety is the fear of being away from a main caregiver, most commonly, a child's mother. Children with separation anxiety become very upset when they have to separate from their main caregiver for any reason. In severe cases they may follow the parent from room to room so as not even to be out of their parent's sight. More commonly, these children will avoid going to school, get upset when their parents try to go out, refuse to sleep over at other people's houses, and try to keep their parents with them at all times. Some children will report stomachaches or other physical problems when they separate, and many will throw tantrums when separation is threatened. The reason for this behavior seems to be a fear that something terrible will happen to the parent or the child while they are apart and that, consequently, they will never see each other again. Lashi, who we introduced earlier, developed separation anxiety after her parents separated, but many children don't have such an obvious trigger.

Generalized Anxiety

Generalized anxiety is a general tendency to be worried or anxious about many areas of life. These children are often described by their parents as "worrywarts." They worry about many general problems such as health, schoolwork, sport performance, bills, burglaries, and even their parents' jobs. They are particularly concerned about any new or novel situation they have to face and will often go to their parents repeatedly to ask questions and to seek reassurance. Many parents report that television shows such as the evening news or police dramas will send their child into a fit of worrying for days. Kurt and Jess, who we introduced earlier, have generalized anxiety.

Social Anxiety or Social Phobia

Social anxiety or social phobia refers to fear and worry in situations where the child has to interact with other people or be the focus of attention. These children are more commonly described as shy, and the central problem is a fear that other people will think badly of them in some way. As a result, they may avoid many situations that involve interaction with other people, including meeting new people, talking on the telephone, joining teams or clubs, answering questions in class, or wearing the "wrong" clothes. George, who we mentioned earlier, has social anxiety.

Obsessive-Compulsive Disorder

In obsessive-compulsive disorder, the child will usually repeat certain actions or thoughts over and over again, often for long periods. Children with obsessive-compulsive problems may have particular thoughts or themes that play on their mind again and again. For example, they may worry about dirt or germs continuously, or they may continually be worried about keeping things orderly and neat. In addition, these children will usually perform some actions repeatedly, often in a superstitious or ritualistic way. For example, they may wash repeatedly in a particular pattern for long periods of time, or they may organize and reorganize their belongings in a very specific pattern. Kurt's main problem is one of obsessive-compulsive disorder.

Panic Disorder

Panic disorder is a fear or worry about having panic attacks. Panic attacks involve a sudden rush of fear that comes with a number of physical symptoms (including racing heart, sweating, dizziness, tingling, and breathlessness). During a panic attack, children may believe that they are dying or that something terrible is happening to them. Panic disorder is not common in young children and is more likely to be found in older adolescents and young adults. Sometimes these adolescents will begin to avoid many situations because of their panic attacks, and, in these cases, the problem is referred to as panic disorder with agoraphobia.

To give you an example—Rosanne was fifteen when she experienced her first panic attack. She was at a friend's party when she began to feel dizzy and sick. Her vision became blurry, and everything seemed to be happening from a long way off. Rosanne was convinced she was going to faint and yelled at her friends to call an ambulance. Many medical tests failed to find any physical problems, but from that time on, Rosanne began to be very afraid of any situations—such as flickering lights, fairground rides, or even exercise—that caused strange feelings in her body. Rosanne continues to have panicky feelings from time to time and is now starting to limit her life and avoids going anywhere that she fears might set off another attack.

Post-Traumatic Stress Disorder

Post-traumatic stress disorder is a reaction to a serious traumatic event in which the child was extremely afraid or injured. Events that might trigger such reactions include car accidents, natural disasters, sexual abuse, or being involved in a burglary. Most children will show some anxiety for a few weeks after a traumatic event. Usually, this reaction gradually disappears. However, in some cases, the reaction continues for many months or even years. Children may keep remembering the event or have bad dreams about it, perhaps even including the trauma in their play. They may suddenly act or feel as if the event is happening again and become very upset. They'll often try hard to avoid situations that remind them of the trauma and may become distant in their feelings. They may show jumpiness, sleep difficulties, and irritability.

To give you an example—Danny is nine years old. When he was eight-and-a-half, he and his father were involved in a car accident. They were stopped at the head of a line of cars waiting at the traffic lights on a busy main road. All of a sudden, the driver of a car coming toward them lost control of his vehicle. Danny watched in terror as the car came toward him and crashed straight into the front of their car. He felt utterly helpless. Although he and his father both recovered physically from the accident, the emotional impact of the accident on Danny remains severe. Danny is often irritable and throws tantrums regularly, something he never did before. Many nights, he wakes in fright as he relives the terror of the accident. He is frightened of traveling in cars and often panics when stopped at traffic lights on busy intersections.

PARENT ACTIVITY: MY CHILD'S ANXIETY

When reading through the descriptions of other children's anxiety, you probably thought to yourself, "That's my son" or "That's my daughter." Thinking about the similarities and differences between these examples and your own child will help you to identify which major areas are difficult for your child. This will help you to think about possible goals and areas to focus on.

Highlight each issue that you think describes a "problem" for your child—in other words, something that interferes with your child's life in some way more than it does for most children his or her age.

SOCIAL FEARS

Shy

Has difficulty meeting people

Has difficulty joining in groups

Has few friends

Avoids interacting with peers

Doesn't like to be the center of attention

Believes others will think badly of him or her

Avoids wearing different clothes

Doesn't speak to people

Scared of asking or answering questions in class

Worries that someone will laugh at him or her or that he or she will be embarrassed

---

SEPARATION FEARS

Worries about getting lost

Worries about someone close to him or her getting hurt or sick

Gets upset when he or she has to be away from Mom or Dad

Gets upset when parents go out

Avoids going to school

Refuses to sleep at other people's homes unless parents are there

Complains of feeling sick when he or she must separate

Afraid of something terrible happening to Mom or Dad (e.g., they may be in a car accident)

GENERALIZED WORRIES

Is extremely conscientious

Worries about making mistakes

Has difficulty performing in exams

Worries about schoolwork or performing well enough

Worries about money, bills, family, health, or safety

Is afraid of new situations

Asks lots of questions or often seeks reassurance

Worries a lot after seeing news programs or scary movies

OBSESSIVE-COMPULSIVE FEARS

Does the same thing over and over again

Complains of thoughts that get "stuck" in his or her mind

Worries continuously about germs or being dirty

Has to do or keep things in a certain order and very precisely

Does a certain action in a ritualistic way

Gets very upset if he or she can't perform ritual

PHYSICAL SYMPTOMS

Complains about feeling sick or stomachaches

Complains about headaches

Has difficulty sleeping

Has fast heartbeat or breathing

Fidgets or paces

Shakes

PANIC FEARS

Has sudden attacks of panic out of the blue

Avoids activities that might make him or her breathless

Thinks that he or she is dying or that something physical is wrong with him or her

Is scared of having more attacks

POST-TRAUMATIC FEARS

Has had a serious traumatic event in the past

Has bad dreams about the event

Can't stop thinking about the event

Becomes very upset when he or she thinks about the event

Avoids situations that remind him or her about it

Is very jumpy and irritable

SPECIFIC FEARS

Avoids very specific things that he or she is afraid of

Is afraid of the dark, heights, insects, animals, doctors, dentists, storms, or water

If confronted with feared object, becomes panicky

Look for themes where you seem to have a lot of marks under one heading. You may find that there are several marks under the physical symptoms list as these are very common across all of the anxiety areas. Then you will find one, two, or three other areas that seem to have more marks than not. With children, it is very common for there to be more than one area that causes problems. Or there might be a few marks in other areas, but there will be one area that is definitely the main problem.

Which areas appear to be problems for your child?

1. _____

2. _____

3. _____

WHY IS YOUR CHILD ANXIOUS?

No one knows the complete answer to this question. But research has identified a number of factors that are likely to play a role in some way. The following sections discuss some of the things that might cause or at least keep anxiety going in children.

Genes

There is little doubt that anxiety runs in families. People who are anxious can often identify some close relative who always seems to be anxious, and it's pretty common for at least one parent of anxious children to also be somewhat anxious. In some cases, this might involve a serious level of anxiety, while in others it might simply be that a parent tends to worry a little more than average. This is particularly likely to be seen in children with higher levels of anxiety. Children with only a single, specific phobia are much less likely to have anxious parents.

Research has shown that what is passed on from parent to child is not a specific tendency to be shy or to worry about the dark, but a general personality that is more emotionally sensitive than other people's. Just as people vary in how tall they are or the color of their hair, people vary in how generally emotional they are. Anxious children tend to have a personality that is more emotional than the average. A large part of this is due to their genes. On the positive side, this means that they are likely to be more caring, kind, honest, and loving. But on the negative side, this emotionality means that they are more likely to worry, brood, feel down, and be fearful. There are both positives and negatives to any child's personality, and we can't and don't want to change these. But the techniques in this book will show you how your child can learn to control some of the things that really interfere with his or her life.

Negative Thoughts

Once a child is anxious and has a "sensitive style," the ways that he or she thinks and behaves play an extremely important part in keeping the anxiety going. In fact, these thoughts and behaviors are the keys to understanding your child's anxiety, and we will focus the main part of the program on helping your child to change these patterns. First, anxious children mentally focus on any possible danger in the world. This includes physical danger (e.g., my parents will die; we will go broke) and social danger (e.g., other kids will laugh at me; I will make a mistake). Anxious children focus on these types of beliefs, often misinterpret unclear events as dangerous, focus their attention on any possible danger, and remember all the bad things, forgetting the good. Importantly, these ways of thinking keep their anxiety going because the world always seems like a dangerous place. Take the case of ten-year-old Kurt, who we described above. Kurt was constantly thinking about his parents getting sick or hurt, about making mistakes in his homework, and about his dog starving to death. In addition, he was always asking his parents about things that could go wrong, and if you asked Kurt about his last school test, he would always remember it as a negative experience. If Kurt heard a noise outside the house, he would assume it was something terrible. Because of all these thoughts and interpretations, the world really did seem like a very terrible place to poor Kurt, and it is no wonder that he was always scared.

Avoiding

Anxious children avoid things. This is a basic and automatic part of their personality—to run away. This might include obvious avoidance like not wanting to go to school or to a party, or it might include less obvious avoidance, such as working really hard on their homework so they never make a mistake or taking ages to decide what to wear so that they don't look bad: *But avoiding—whether it is obvious or subtle—is the key to keeping anxiety alive.* Avoiding keeps the thoughts that we described above real because children never learn that those thoughts are not true. By avoiding anything that is a little frightening, children are not able to learn positive lessons such as, "I can cope," "It's not that bad," or "It won't hurt me." Take the case of George whose main problem involves believing that other people will think he is stupid or incompetent. George would avoid talking to kids, would stay quiet and "hidden" in groups, and would make excuses not to talk on the phone or ask people for advice. But by avoiding all these things in both obvious and subtle ways, George was never able to learn that people would not think he is incompetent.

Parent Reaction

The way you react to or handle your child's fears might also play some part in maintaining the anxiety. While all parents differ, some parents react to their anxious child in an overly protective way. This is very understandable. Parents love their children and so when faced with a child who is scared, vulnerable, and worried, parents only too naturally rush to his or her aid. But, in some cases, this helping behavior allows the child to avoid. Some parents begin to anticipate their child's anxiety and will start to help their child even when it isn't necessary. This is especially the case if the parent is also anxious. If this pattern becomes established, the child is not forced to face his or her fears and as a result may begin to learn that "The world really is dangerous" and "I cannot handle it myself."

Parent Modeling

There is little doubt that children copy their parents. Just think of the young girl who walks out of Mommy's room covered in makeup, wearing high heels and jewelry. It is reasonable, then, to expect that children may also copy their parents' ways of coping with the world. If a parent is anxious and copes by avoiding situations, then the child may learn that this is the way to handle fears. We are not saying that you are entirely responsible for your child's anxiety; there is no way that modeling could explain even the majority of anxious behavior. But if your child already has some anxious tendencies and either you or your partner is anxious, your child may pick up a few of these behaviors, and this may strengthen his or her already anxious nature.

Stressors

When a child is bitten by a dog, the child will become wary of dogs for a period of time. When a child's parents separate and divorce, the child will often lose some confidence and become more sensitive for a time. These are natural responses that happen to most children after a stressful event. If a child experiences stressors like these and is already sensitive and anxious, then these stressors may have an even bigger impact than usual and may add to his or her anxiety. Common stressors include parental separation, family violence, death of a loved one, being bullied at school, doing badly in school, getting sick, and specific incidents (e.g., being in a car accident, being robbed, being bitten or stung, and being in a fire). Experiences like these cannot be identified in all or even the majority of cases of anxiety. But they may be important in triggering anxiety in some children.

In addition, we are starting to learn that people often create their own stressors. It appears that the very fears and worries that anxious children have can often lead to more stress in their lives, and this can increase their anxiety. For example, an anxious child may have some unusual behaviors that, in turn, lead other children to tease him or her. Or an anxious child may stop his or her parents going out at night, which may increase pressure on the parents and then lead to more tension in the family.

PARENT ACTIVITY: ANXIOUS FACTORS FOR MY CHILD

We have described several factors that probably help to keep your child feeling anxious and worried. Not all of these factors will be important for every child. However, avoidance is the key and is a part of any anxiety problem.

Have a look at the parent activity worksheet on the next page. It lists some of the main factors that we have been discussing. See if you can put in some of the points from your own child's life that might show which factors are important to your child.

We cannot emphasize enough that this activity is not an exercise in self-blame. It has been an observation of many therapists that parents want to know at least a bit about the causes of anxiety, but when it comes down to the crunch, it doesn't matter where it came from; what matters is that we can do something about it!

YOUR CHILD'S ANXIETY

GENES

Family member(s) who you would describe as somewhat "emotional" or "nervous"

_____

ANXIOUS BELIEFS

Key themes that your child worries about or "danger" that he or she focuses on

_____

_____

PARENT REACTION

Situations where you help your child, or allow him or her to not participate, to reduce your child's fears

_____

_____

AVOIDANCE

Actions your child does or does not do because of anxiety?

_____

_____

STRESSORS

Events in your child's life that might increase his or her fears?

_____

_____

MAIN FEARS

(What are the main things your child is scared of?)

_____

_____

_____

HOW CAN YOU HELP YOUR ANXIOUS CHILD?

The skills you will learn in this program will all be aimed at the factors that we have just been talking about. Each of the skills and techniques for managing anxiety that your child will learn are aimed at some part of this model. Even if you don't believe that one of the factors is important for your child's anxiety, it may still help your child to learn that skill. So we strongly suggest that you and your child work on every one of the skills in this program.

To get a better idea of how it all fits together, see the following illustration, which shows you how each of the skills your child will learn fits with each of the factors that we have been talking about that maintain anxiety. We have included the name of the skill that we will be using for each factor in italics. As you can see, the key skill is to get your child to gradually and consistently face the things he or she is afraid of (see the discussion of stepladders in chapter 5). However, all of the other skills will help to improve and add to this skill so that the whole program works together.

CHANGING CHILD ANXIETY

GENES

Okay—we can't change this part yet, but it does tell you that some of these patterns are simply part of the way your child is.

ANXIOUS BELIEFS

Using *realistic thinking*, your child will learn to think realistically and focus less on danger.

PARENT REACTION

Using *parent management skills*, you and your partner will learn to allow your child to become more independent.

AVOIDANCE

Using *stepladders*, your child will gradually begin to do more and more things that he or she currently tries to avoid.

STRESSORS

By practicing *social skills* and *assertiveness*, your child will learn to cope better with situations that are stressful.

YOUR CHILD'S MAIN FEARS

At the end of the program, your child should be more calm and confident, and fears and worries should no longer rule his or her life.

Putting Together a Program for Your Child

Every child is different, and there is no single program or set of skills that will suit each child. If you work with a professional therapist, it is his or her job to help tailor and fit the best program for your child's unique situation. If you are going to work through this program mostly by yourself, then you will need to do this. You may want to read ahead to see how the different skills and techniques that we cover in this program work together. Toward the end of the book, in chapter 9, we provide a detailed description of the specific programs that were used by each of the sample children whose stories we described earlier. It is a good idea for you to skip ahead and have a quick look at how these different programs are put together. To give you another view of the program, we describe below the structure that we use in our standard clinical program that we run at Macquarie University in Sydney, Australia. This program is run in ten sessions that are spread over twelve weeks. A description of what we cover each week is shown in the table below. This might give you an idea of an approximate timetable for running the program with your child.

MACQUARIE UNIVERSITY *COOL KIDS* PROGRAM FOR MANAGEMENT OF CHILD ANXIETY

What we cover	Chapter in this book	What children practice
Week 1 Understanding anxiety	1 and 2	Linking thoughts and feelings
Week 2 Thinking realistically	3	Detective thinking
Week 3 Thinking realistically, rewards, and managing child behavior	4	Rewards and detective thinking Child management (parents)
Weeks 4 and 5 Stepladders	5	Detective thinking and stepladders
Week 6 Shortcutting detective thinking and advanced stepladders	6	Stepladders (with detective thinking)
Week 7 Troubleshooting stepladders	7	Stepladders (with detective thinking)
Week 8 Social skills	8	Stepladders (with detective thinking) and assertiveness
Weeks 9, 10, and 11 Discuss difficulties and review all techniques	9	Stepladders (with detective thinking) and assertiveness
Week 12 Future goals and coping with setbacks	10	Plans for the future

IN SUMMARY

Anxious children believe that the world is a dangerous place. Because of this belief, they will often interpret very innocent events as examples of danger. For example, a normal noise outside at night might be interpreted as a burglar. In this way, this thinking style can help to maintain anxiety by "showing" the child that their fears are real. Most importantly, anxious children will usually avoid things they fear. Because of this avoidance, they never have an opportunity to find out that what they are scared of probably won't happen and that they can cope if it does. Again, this maintains anxiety by not allowing children to learn that what they fear is usually not true. Where parents allow their children to avoid their anxieties—perhaps by doing things for them and protecting them from possible worry— parents are also allowing these beliefs to stay.

In this program we will help you to teach your child how to think more realistically about the world and to expect less danger in situations; we will teach you different ways of handling and interacting with your child; and we will show you how you can encourage your child to approach the situations he or she fears in a gradual and consistent manner. Together with these strategies, we will also cover some additional techniques that may be of help in some circumstances. These include coping strategies such as improved social skills, assertiveness, and dealing with teasing. At the end of the book, we have included an appendix about relaxation. This is not a key part of our program, but we have included it because some parents and children find relaxation a very useful way of dealing with anxiety and tension.

MOTIVATING YOUR CHILD TO BEGIN THIS PROGRAM

It can be difficult to get anxious children to try anything new. Usually they tend to expect the worst and feel nervous at the thought of having to do something that they haven't tried before. They may worry that the program will be too difficult or that they will be forced to do frightening things that they feel they can't do. Many anxious children also like to try to appear perfect in front of their parents (and peers) and so may have difficulty admitting their limitations. At the same time your child is probably aware of how uncomfortable it feels to be anxious and would most likely prefer to be free of anxiety.

At the same time, starting a program like this can be a little scary for a parent. Working through the anxiety management exercises in this book will not be easy. You will be asked to look at some of your own feelings and behaviors at some points. And you may have to be prepared to make some of your own changes if your child is really going to improve. Above all, working on this program will take time and energy—the program won't work if you or your child are not fully committed.

Therefore, it is important to have your child's full cooperation, and you will also need to make this program your number one priority for the next few months. The program will work best if you and your child see this as a combined adventure. The two of you will need to form a team, working toward some common goals. A good way to encourage your child's cooperation and motivation is to discuss the negative aspects of being anxious and the benefits that might come from learning to control anxiety. Remember—most children love doing things with their parents. If you treat this as a game or adventure that you are going to do together, your child will be much more likely to go along with you.

It is a good idea to sit down with your child and talk about the program you are going to do together. Here are a few points to cover:

- Feeling anxious is normal, and there are many children who feel just the same way.

- You and your child will work on this program together— you are included every step of the way. You might describe it as an adventure in which the two (or three) of you will be a team.

- Your child will not be forced to do anything he or she doesn't want to do.

- New skills will be learned one small step at a time.

- The program will be fun and will also include rewards that can be earned.

- At the end of the program, your child should feel more brave and confident.

Remember that this program will not take away all the normal protective anxieties that a child may have in certain situations (e.g., being scared of walking down a dark alley). Instead, it aims to teach skills to manage the bits of anxiety that are "over the top" and that get in the way of your child doing what he or she wants in life.

Getting the Most Out of the Program—Using the Children's Activities

To get the most out of the program, it is very important that you and your child regularly work on the activities and practice tasks. Reward your child for his or her efforts in completing the work by consistently showing encouragement and interest in what he or she has written. If you stop paying attention to the tasks, your child will very quickly follow. Most children appreciate stamps, small stickers, or tokens that they can cash in later for bigger rewards. Giving your child a star or sticker each time he or she successfully completes an exercise is a good way to help make the program fun and to motivate your child to continue. However, attention and interest from you as well as your praise will be the most powerful rewards and the best ways to motivate your child. We will say more about using rewards later. One really simple principle is the "minute-for-minute exchange"—that is, for every minute your child spends working on the program, he or she gets a minute of an enjoyable activity such as computer time or story time with a parent.

PARENT ACTIVITY: WHAT ARE OUR GOALS?

It's time to think about what you might like to get out of the program. How far you get will depend on how much time you are prepared to put into it and how hard you and your child work at the new skills. Having goals in mind will help boost motivation and can also be used later to see how far you have progressed.

As we said earlier, this parent activity is designed for you, the parent, to do in order to help you to help your child during your anxiety management session together. In that session there will be a children's activity (described below) where your child will get a chance to talk about his or her own goals.

What would you like your child to be able to do, which he or she currently doesn't do because of anxiety (e.g., spend time with a friend after school, catch the bus every day, greet people when they say hello, fall asleep within a half-hour of going to bed, go to summer camp, visit friends who have dogs)?

1. _____

2. _____

3. _____

4. _____

What would you like your child *not to do* and how often does he or she do these things now (e.g., avoid going to school, sleep in your bed, ask questions, get stomachaches—every day, once a week)?

1. _____

2. _____

3. _____

4. _____

List broader goals that *you* would like to achieve (e.g., confidence in reacting to new situations).

_____

_____

_____

_____

We will look back at these goals at the end of the program (in chapter 10) to see how far your child has come and what you still want to achieve.

Finally, can you think of any practical barriers that might get in the way of running this program? For example, your child might be doing too many after-school activities to fit in something else, or you may have a partner who doesn't support this program, and so on.

1. _____

2. _____

3. _____

4. _____

Spend a few minutes thinking about these barriers and then about ways you might try and overcome them. For example, if your child does too many activities after school, there may be another time to try this program that will work better, such as during school holidays.

_____

_____

_____

_____

ACTIVITIES TO DO WITH YOUR CHILD ...

As we mentioned earlier, at the end of each chapter you will find activities to do with your child that will help you to teach anxiety management skills. Each activity will have a set of instructions to help you with what to discuss with your child, and descriptions of worksheets that you will need to create for your child to complete (with your help). You will need to base your discussions on what you read in the chapter and will be able to base your worksheets on the examples within the chapter. Alternatively, you can download a workbook from *www.ceh. mq.edu.au/hyac.html*. This workbook contains all of the activities to print out and use with your child as well as providing child-friendly explanations of each skill and blank worksheets for your child to complete, which will reduce the amount of preparation you need to do before sitting with your child for the anxiety management session. The parent instructions below are repeated in the workbook within each workbook activity.

CHILDREN'S ACTIVITY 1: WHAT IS ANXIETY?

Start off by talking with your child about worries and fears and how being anxious can sometimes be helpful (for example, by getting you scared if you smell smoke in the house or by revving you up for a big test or game).

Explain though that sometimes we get anxious when there really isn't anything to be afraid of, such as getting scared by a noise outside at night that is being made by the next-door neighbor's cat. Some kids, in fact, get a lot more anxious a lot more often than other kids and consequently they miss out on fun activities or spend a lot of time feeling bad.

Tell them about the three parts of anxiety: how the body reacts (e.g., fast heart beat), what the person thinks (e.g., that the dog in the park is dangerous), and what the person does (e.g., leaving the park so that the dog can't get them). Try to use examples to help them to understand that when they feel anxious, they can tell that's how they're feeling by what happens to their body, what they think, and what they do.

Tell them that strong anxiety is common for about one in every ten kids, and explain that some people are more anxious than others partly because they were born that way and partly because they have learned to believe that the world is a dangerous place.

Finally explain that you will spend some time each week doing activities that will help you both to learn how to manage anxiety. Encourage them to ask questions and, if needed, reassure them that you will be working on managing anxiety together and will be taking it nice and slow.

CHILDREN'S ACTIVITY 2: MEET SOME OTHER CHILDREN WITH ANXIETY

Read stories with them about different children who have anxiety, either the ones from earlier in the chapter or from their workbook. Hopefully, this can get you started talking about their own fears and worries and how they are not alone and are not "crazy."

CHILDREN'S ACTIVITY 3: ME AND MY ANXIETY

Talk with your child about his or her own fears and worries. First list all the things that people could be afraid of or worried about (younger children might like to cut out pictures from magazines of the different situations). Then circle each one that you were afraid of when young (or even what worries you now) and then have your child circle each one that he or she finds difficult. Be very careful not to turn this into an "interview" and do not start telling your child to stop worrying about these things. Just accept your child's view and ask questions so that you and your child can understand more about the fear.

CHILDREN'S ACTIVITY 4: MY GOALS

Begin by talking with your child about what he or she might get out of doing the program. A good way to phrase it might be to ask questions like, "Are there things that are hard for you to do now because they make you nervous?" or "Are there things that you would like to do without being scared?" Or you may focus on more concrete positives (especially if you have a younger child), for example, "Would you like to be able to make friends more easily?" While there may be lots of things that you personally want out of the program (like being able to leave your child with a sitter while you go out at night), you need to focus here on what positives your child might get out of the program (like becoming a "big" boy or girl, feeling more brave, and having more friends). Write down the main goals that your child comes up with on some brightly colored paper. It is a good idea to put this somewhere that you and your child will see regularly to remind yourselves of why you are doing the program, especially when things get a little tougher. Encourage your child to decorate these goals and be proud of where he or she is heading.

CHILDREN'S ACTIVITY 5: THE FAMILY COMMITMENT

It is really useful to get your child to make a commitment to the program and to be supported by the family. Hopefully your child will want to continue with the program after talking about how things might be better without anxiety. A family commitment like this can really help to show how serious the next few months will be and how hard you and your child are going to have to work.

Create a contract for your child and you to sign (a pre-prepared contract is included in the workbook). The contract should state that you and your child (and any other person helping with the program) are going to learn to manage anxiety together and that you will work together once a week and a little bit each day to make this happen. You can write into the contract any reward that will be given for working each week on the program (for example, an extra hour on the computer).

You should plan a special activity that those signing the contract will do at the end of the program. This activity should be just for the parents and the child doing the program. The point is to make your child feel special and that his or her (and your) hard work is going to be rewarded. We suggest allowing three months to complete the program. The removal or loss of this activity should never be used as a threat during the program, but it can be used as a means of motivating everyone to remember that working on the anxiety is a commitment that will have benefits in the long run.

This contract represents your family commitment to the program. None of you should sign it if you do not want to commit. If your child is hesitant or does not want to commit, try to talk through why this is. It is likely that your child is afraid of what he or she will be made to do. After all, none of us likes to be made to do things we don't want to do. You might begin by reminding your child of the positives he or she will get out of the program—in other words, the goals that will be reached. Then let your child know that he or she will be part of the program at every step and so will have a big say in exactly what and when to do things. If this still doesn't work, you may need to write a "partial contract." In other words, write a contract to commit only to the next few weeks, or, if necessary, even just the next week. If a short-term contract is needed, weekly rewards for working on the program will most likely be needed as well. If you can get your child to agree to at least begin, hopefully he or she will find it more fun as things move along.

CHAPTER HIGHLIGHTS

In this chapter, you and your child learned ...

- That you can identify problematic fears by examining the impact that anxiety has on everyday life

- How anxiety affects three aspects of a person: their thoughts, their body, and their behavior

- That anxiety can be divided into several different types and that it is common for children to experience difficulties in more than one area

- That there are different factors that can cause or maintain anxiety, including genes, negative thinking, avoiding, parent reactions, parent modeling, and stressors

- How each anxiety management skill is targeted at a particular factor that keeps anxiety going

Your child will need to do the following:

- Complete the children's activities with the help of a parent or other adult.

- Set goals and make a commitment to learning to manage anxiety.

CHAPTER 2

How Do Thoughts and Feelings Affect Anxiety?

THE FIRST STEPS TOWARD LEARNING ANXIETY MANAGEMENT SKILLS

There are some simple pieces of information that can really help children learn to manage their anxiety better. Younger children might need to spend a little more time in this section, whereas older children might cover it fairly quickly.

Learning About Feelings

Many children have difficulty in naming feelings and in being able to describe the differences between emotions. It's important to make sure that your child understands and can recognize different emotions before moving on to teach ways of controlling anxiety. You can help your child by labeling and discussing feelings in everyday situations and by playing games based on feelings. The first children's activity for this week shows some different emotions to get you started. You might also try some other ways to get your child to think about different feelings. For example, play a game where your child acts out a feeling, first just being given the name of the feeling (e.g., sad, angry) and then being given a situation (e.g., winning a prize, losing a wallet). Your child then acts out the feeling he or she would probably have in that situation. Try to make it fun and silly. If the rest of the family is willing to get involved, you can make a set of cards or pieces of paper with different feelings written on them and have each person take turns in picking one of the cards and acting out that feeling without using words. Other members of the family can then try to guess what the feeling is.

Your child should learn that there are several different forms of anxiety. For example, fear, worry, tension, shyness, embarrassment, and terror all have a focus on possible danger at their core. While there may be slight differences between them, as far as this program is concerned, they are all basically the same.

The Worry Scale

An important step is to teach your child how to measure his or her fears. This will help your child understand that strong emotions do not come from nowhere or "out of the blue." In addition, your child needs to learn that we are not trying to "get rid of" anxiety, but are simply teaching him or her to control it better. So being able to distinguish between different levels of fear will become important later in the program.

We use the worry scale to show different degrees or levels of anxiety. In activity 7 you will teach your child about this scale. The thermometer uses a scale from 0 to 10 on which different levels of anxiety are marked from 0 (very relaxed) to 10 (extremely worried). This is a personal judgment, and everyone will have different perceptions for different situations. What is important is that your child learns to recognize that anxiety is not an all-or-nothing feeling but can vary in degree.

After teaching your child about the worry scale (using this chapter's activities), it is important to have your child practice giving worry-scale ratings. Ask your child how anxious he or she is in different situations through the day. This will help your child to become more aware of his or her anxiety levels and will also give the two of you a common language to use to describe anxiety (e.g., "I feel at 4 now" or "I'm at 7 at the moment").

How Anxiety Affects Your Child

We have already described for you how anxiety can affect a person. We discussed the idea that anxiety affects three different aspects of a person—body, behavior, and thoughts. It is also important for your child to develop an understanding of this lesson by becoming aware of how anxiety affects him or her. At your anxiety management session for this week, begin by teaching your child about how anxiety might affect him or her across the three systems—physical symptoms, thoughts, and behaviors. Some of the information you might cover follows.

HOW ANXIETY AFFECTS THE BODY

When we become frightened, our body goes through many changes. These may include any of the following:

- Breathing fast
- Butterflies in tummy
- Needing to go to the toilet
- Wobbly knees
- Tense muscles
- Dizziness
- Crying
- Sweating
- Stomachache
- Shakiness

- Headache

- Feeling too hot

- Fidgetiness

- Increasing heart rate

- Blushing

You can begin to get younger children to think about these changes by asking them to think of a frightened animal such as a cat. Ask what physical changes would happen if a cat was asleep and woke up suddenly to see a dog standing next to it (e.g., fur standing up, big eyes, tensed-up body, and scared expression). After this you can ask your child to think about how his or her own body feels during anxious times. It is often useful if you or other family members are willing to discuss what happens to your and their bodies when anxious, to show both the similarities and the differences in how people react to anxiety. Activity 8 at the end of this chapter will help you and your child identify these reactions.

HOW ANXIETY AFFECTS THOUGHTS

It is also going to be important for your child to become more aware of his or her worried thoughts and beliefs. In fact this is one of the more important parts of this section since you will be moving on in later weeks to help your child change his or her anxious thoughts. Your child will learn that certain feelings go along with certain thoughts and that anxious feelings tend to go along with thoughts of danger. In addition, your child needs to begin to become more aware of the particular bad things that he or she tends to expect. When teaching your child about thoughts, try to get him or her to suggest thoughts that indicate some sort of event rather than simply describing the feeling. For example, a thought such as, "This is going to hurt" is good because it describes a bad outcome that a person might be expecting. However, a thought such as, "I am scared," which simply describes the feeling, doesn't tell you anything about what your child is scared about. One of the hardest things for children in this part of the program is to learn the difference between thoughts and feelings, so it is best to try not to confuse these things. It is a good idea to introduce the term "worried thoughts" here. Your child should begin to understand that when we feel scared, nervous, or shy, it is because we have some sort of worried thought or belief. Of course sometimes these worried thoughts might be quite hard to identify, and some children will say "I just feel that way." If your child does this, don't push it yet. It is enough in this case to get your child to "guess" what he or she might be thinking. The concept of worried thoughts will become important later in the program.

HOW ANXIETY AFFECTS BEHAVIOR

It is a good idea to get your child to think about how he or she behaves or acts when anxious. This is likely to include different ways of avoiding or escaping from the frightening situation but may also include other behaviors such as pacing, hitting, throwing tantrums, asking for help, or biting nails. To try to raise your child's awareness of what he or she typically does when anxious, first tell your child what you do, then ask what he or she thinks someone else in the family does, before finally asking what it is that he or she typically does. As with worried thoughts, some children may not recognize or admit to all their behaviors. Again, don't push too hard at this stage.

PARENT ACTIVITY: LEARNING ABOUT MY CHILD'S ANXIETY PATTERNS

Since you are going to be helping your child through this program, it is a good idea for you to learn a little more about these patterns as well.

To help with this, on a separate piece of paper, create a table with the headings "Situation," "What does my child usually say or ask?" "What doesn't my child do because of fear or worry?" and "What does my child think will happen?" Then, over the next few days, watch your child carefully—keeping in mind his or her anxious behaviors, thoughts, and feelings—and complete the table.

Based on the gathered information, what is it about your child that alerts you to the fact that he or she is worried or scared (think about typical things he or she says, physical symptoms, mood swings, etc.)?

_____

_____

_____

_____

_____

_____

_____

_____

_____

_____

_____

_____

This information will also be helpful during later activities, so keep it handy.

LINKING SITUATIONS, THOUGHTS, AND FEELINGS

Once your child has learned the different ways that anxiety affects him or her, the next step in the program is to help children to understand that there is a link between a situation, their thoughts, and how they are feeling. To do this successfully, your child will need to be able to identify situations that he or she has been in, what he or she thought during that time, and how he or she was feeling in that situation. This is the first skill that will require a short period of daily practice before your child will be able to confidently identify thoughts separate from his or her feelings.

We use a form to help children record the link between situations, thoughts, and feelings. The following is a completed example. The form asks children to describe the situation that made them frightened, their thoughts at the time, how they actually felt (e.g., frightened, worried, shy, nervous, etc.), and the degree of fear or worry on the worry scale.

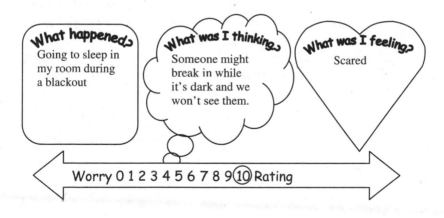

What happened? Going to sleep in my room during a blackout

What was I thinking? Someone might break in while it's dark and we won't see them.

What was I feeling? Scared

Worry 0 1 2 3 4 5 6 7 8 9 (10) Rating

ACTIVITIES TO DO WITH YOUR CHILD ...

CHILDREN'S ACTIVITY 6: LEARNING ABOUT FEELINGS

Use a magazine with many pictures of people in it (*National Geographic* is very good for this or use the cartoon faces provided in the workbook at www.ceh .mq.edu.ua/hyac.html) to start a conversation on the different types of feelings that people can have. Try to encourage your child to use a variety of feeling words. After naming many feelings, play a game of feelings charades: concentrate on using body language and facial expressions to express feelings, and have your child guess the feeling as well as act ones out for you. To get started, write feelings on pieces of paper and take turns pulling them out of a hat.

CHILDREN'S ACTIVITY 7: THE WORRY SCALE

Show your child the worry-scale thermometer included on the next page or in the workbook. Explain to your child that sometimes we only feel a little bit worried, but at other times we feel really, really scared. So that we can tell other people how scared we are very quickly, we can rate the feeling of worry on a worry scale, just like you can read the temperature on a thermometer. Have your child use the worry scale to describe his or her degree of worry in a list of different situations, including silly ones (like waking up and finding that a lion is in the bed), ones that are likely to get a very low rating (such as visiting Grandma for her birthday), and situations that you know your child finds very frightening. Make sure your child is giving ratings across the range on the worry scale.

The Worry Scale

10   Extremely Worried

9

8   Very Worried

7

6   Worried

5

4   A Bit Worried

3

2   Not Sure

1

0   Very Relaxed

Reprinted with permission from the Centre for Emotional Health, Macquarie University, Sydney, Australia.

Children's Activity 8: Anxiety and My Body

Create an outline of a body that your child can use to show where anxiety affects him or her. You may choose to draw one freehand, but a fun alternative is to get a huge sheet of paper, have your child lie on it, and then draw an outline of your child with a pen on the paper. Your child can then use this personal "portrait" to color and show where and how anxiety affects him or her. If needed, use the list from the section "How Anxiety Affects the Body" to remind your child of possible body symptoms. Help your child feel okay about these symptoms by comparing them to the ones that you get when worried or scared.

Children's Activity 9: How Anxiety Affects My Thoughts

Talk with your child about how feelings depend on what you are thinking. Look at magazine pictures and ask your child how the person is feeling and then have him or her guess what that person might be thinking. Using pictures of situations that could be either positive or negative, such as a child ice skating (cartoons of these situations are provided in the workbook). Ask your child to identify a thought that would make the person feel happy and then a thought that might make the person feel worried or scared. You may need to do this several times for your child to easily identify thoughts for different situations. At the end of the activity, point out how different people can have different thoughts and that even the same person can have different thoughts about one situation.

Children's Activity 10: Linking Thoughts and Feelings

Draw a table with the headings "What happened?" "What was I thinking?" "What was I feeling?" or pictures similar to the square, thought bubble, and heart in the picture on page 53. Then ask your child to think of a time when he or she felt really happy and relaxed and to think about where he or she was, who was there too, and what they were doing. Write a short description of the situation in the first box. Now ask your child to try to remember what he or she was thinking or saying to him- or herself in his or her head. This might be a bit hard to remember if the situation happened a long time ago. If your child can't remember exactly what he or she was thinking, try to guess what it might have been in that situation. Write this in the "What was I thinking?" box. Then ask your child to indicate how he or she was feeling. Write this in the "What was I feeling?" box. Finally, have your child rate how worried he or she was in this situation using the worry scale (probably 0).

Next, repeat this exercise having your child think of a time when he or she felt terribly worried or afraid. Finally have your child describe a situation that has happened in the past day or two and ask your child to tell you what he or she was thinking and feeling. You may complete several examples from the past few days to help your child understand that thoughts are related to feelings.

Children's Practice Task 1: Learning About My Thoughts and Feelings

As we said before, it's important for your child to learn to become more aware of his or her own patterns of anxiety. You can do this by having your child keep a record of his or her anxiety for a week or two, recording a number of examples of situations, thoughts, and feelings that bothered him or her. Use a picture or table like the one in activity 10 and have your child make an entry on the sheet whenever he or she feels anxious, worried, shy, or scared, even if only a little. This may be many times a day or only once a day. But you should try to encourage your child to make at least one entry each day. Remember to praise and reward your child for these efforts during the week.

CHAPTER HIGHLIGHTS

In this chapter, you and your child learned …

- How to recognize and distinguish between different types of feelings

- How to use the worry scale to rate the intensity of anxious feelings

- What happens to your body when you are anxious

- That in each situation where you feel anxious, you have a worried thought that causes the bad feeling

Your child will need to do the following:

- Complete the children's activities with the help of a parent or other adult.

- Complete Practice Task 1. Fill out the table that you put together in activity 10 at least once per day for at least one week. (A worksheet for Practice Task 1 is provided in the workbook on the Internet at *www.ceh.mq.edu.au/hyac.html* and is called "Learning About My Thoughts and Feelings.")

CHAPTER 3

Learning to Think Realistically

Learning to think more realistically is a very useful strategy to help any person, adult or child, master anxiety. It will be particularly helpful as a part of your child's program. However it is not an easy technique to use properly, even for adults. Therefore, in order to be able to really help your child use this skill, it is best if you can learn to use it yourself. For this reason, we have written this chapter in two parts. In the first part, we teach the ideas and methods of realistic thinking to you so that you can fully understand how it works. Because it is a complex technique, we recommend that you also use realistic thinking in your own life for a while to help you with any situations of worry, stress, or anger. Putting it into practice in this way will help you to better understand how it works. In the second part of the chapter, we show you how you can teach realistic thinking to your child, calling it "detective thinking" and making it a little simpler to learn than the full technique that you will be using.

If you have identified some fears and worries in your own life, then learning to use the realistic thinking strategy and allowing your child to see and hear you using it, will be especially important.

THE BASICS OF REALISTIC THINKING

Before you can learn to change your thoughts, and in that way manage your feelings as well as help your child, there are some basic principles that you need to understand.

The Relationship Between Events, Thoughts, and Feelings

Most people think that events happening outside of themselves cause feelings. In other words, if you experience a certain event, then certain feelings will be the inevitable result. For example, how many times have you said, "*You* made me so angry" or "That noise scared me"? However, outside events such as traffic jams or the actions of another person cannot be fully responsible for your feelings. One way to understand this is to realize that two people can experience exactly the same event and feel differently about it. The same person can also experience the same event at different times and feel quite differently about it at each time. Why is this?

The answer lies in the content of your beliefs, thoughts, or self-talk—in other words, your feelings depend on what you are telling yourself about an event. As you will see in the following examples, your beliefs about a situation or event determine how you will feel about that situation or event.

Imagine that both Tony's wife and Jim's wife are an hour late in coming home from the movies. Tony tells himself that his wife probably decided to have a coffee with her friend (this is his belief about the situation). As a result of holding this belief, he is not concerned about her, although he is somewhat annoyed that she didn't think to call and let him know. Jim, on the other hand, tells himself that his wife must have been involved in a car accident (this is his belief about the situation). As a direct result of holding this belief, he is worried sick.

This example clearly demonstrates that it is not the situation per se (wife being late) that results in the emotions experienced by each man. Instead, it's the beliefs or thoughts held by each that are responsible for the different reactions. The event might act as a trigger, but the emotion that the trigger prompts depends on how the event is *interpreted* by the person. Let's look at another example in which we can see different emotions experienced by the same individual, apparently in response to the same situation.

Celine has just finished a hard day's work and she is feeling tired and irritable. She gets home just as her husband, Aaron, is feeding their young son, Charles. When Aaron leaves for a few minutes, Charles begins playing with his food and, laughing, suddenly picks up the bowl and puts the whole meal on top of his head. He thinks this is hilarious, but Celine is furious about the mess. On another night, exactly the same thing happens. But this time, Celine has just been given a promotion at work and is feeling pretty good. This time, when Charles tips the bowl over his head, Celine thinks it is the cutest thing and laughs along. Here again, we can see an example of two different emotions being triggered by the same event. But this time it is happening in the same person. The difference lies entirely in what is going on inside Celine's head. In one case, Celine thinks about the mess and the inconvenience and becomes angry. In the other case, Celine thinks how cute her son is and how much fun he is having and she feels good.

Although it is tempting to believe that an event itself determines the way in which we react to it, in actual fact, our beliefs and thoughts based on our interpretations of that event directly determine how we react. As you and your child work through this program, try to remind yourself that our emotions are not directly caused by the things that go on around us. Instead, our feelings and emotions are the direct result of the way that we *think about*, or *interpret*, events and situations. Here is an example:

EVENT	BELIEF/THOUGHT	FEELING
Hear	"The dog's been run over."	Panic
screeching	"Those hoodlums are at it again."	Anger
brakes	"Lucky they missed"	Relief

Two Common Errors in Thinking

Most people who worry a lot or feel stressed tend to make two errors in their thinking. First, they commonly overestimate how likely it is that bad events will occur. Second, they usually assume that the outcomes or consequences of those events will be catastrophic and unbearable.

1. OVERESTIMATING PROBABILITY

Someone who is an anxious person often believes that bad things are very likely to happen to them, even though this may not be true. Think, for example, of someone who is very shy, having to get up and give a speech at a wedding. They might well think, "I just know that I am going to say the wrong thing." Now it is possible that this person will end up saying something a little inappropriate. But it's quite hard to say the wrong thing at a wedding, and the chance that that person will say the wrong thing is probably not very high. Thinking, "I am going to say the wrong thing" implies 100 percent probability—that is, that you will definitely say the wrong thing. Clearly, this is an overestimate.

Similarly, if you're late coming home, your child would feel anxious if he or she believes, "Mom and Dad have had an accident." But this thought again implies 100 percent probability—"Mom and Dad have definitely had an accident." While there may be some chance that you have had an accident, the reality is that it is probably pretty unlikely. So if your child is thinking that it is definite, that is an overestimate that only serves to intensify anxiety.

2. OVERESTIMATING CONSEQUENCES

To highly stressed people, life often seems very threatening. Not only do they believe that unpleasant things are highly likely to happen to them, they also believe that if those things do happen, the consequences will be absolutely catastrophic and intolerable.

Interestingly, most people who assume the worst are unaware they are doing it. In other words, they typically have never asked themselves the question, "What's the worst thing that could happen, and could I cope if it did happen?" For instance, imagine that you are on your way to an appointment. As you sit in your car, stuck in traffic, you think to yourself, "Oh no, I'm going to be really late." As part of this thought, you are assuming that being late will be really terrible.

In other words, you are saying to yourself, "I am going to be late, and that is the end of the world." But if you could ask yourself the question, "If I am late, what will really happen and will I be able to cope with that?" you will probably find that being late is not really as tragic as you are assuming.

As another example, imagine that your child is very anxious about making a mistake on his or her homework. As part of this fear, he or she is probably assuming that making a mistake will be the "end of the world." In fact, while the teacher may make a comment about it, making a mistake in homework will probably have no serious effects at all. This shows you the second type of common problem in thinking—overestimating the negative consequences of things.

CHANGING YOUR BELIEFS

So if our feelings come directly from our beliefs about a situation, and anxious people tend to believe that bad things are more likely to happen to them than they really are, it seems reasonable that if we could change those beliefs, we could control our anxiety to some extent.

Before we go any further, we need to point out an important limitation. No one can ever control their thoughts and beliefs 100 percent and so no one is going to be able to control their feelings 100 percent. That is not what we want to do. What we are aiming for is to teach you how you can help your child to control his or her *extreme* beliefs to a *small* degree. By doing this, your child will also be able to reduce the extreme emotions to a small degree. This is one small step in learning to overcome anxiety.

The answer to reducing extreme anxiety is to learn how you might change your beliefs from extreme ones to less extreme ones. For example, instead of thinking, "My partner has been in a car accident and he or she has been killed," you need to think, "There is a chance that my partner has been in a car accident, but it is more likely that there is another reason for his or her lateness, and even if he or she has had an accident, it's probably not a huge one." If you believed the second thought, your anxiety would diminish.

The key to changing your emotions is belief. In other words, there is no point in simply saying to yourself, "My partner hasn't been killed in a car accident" if you don't believe it. You have to convince yourself that the less extreme thought is true. Luckily, in most cases it is, and so it is usually not too hard to think of the less extreme thought. In most cases in life, the extreme, catastrophic belief is just not very realistic. Usually, the less extreme belief is the more realistic one. That is why we call this technique *realistic thinking*. (*Note:* when explaining it to your child, you might want to call it *detective thinking,* which we will describe later in this chapter.) Most people who are anxious tend to think in unrealistic ways. By learning to think more realistically, they can learn to control their anxiety.

Of course, an important point that this raises is that at times, things will happen in life that are bad. At these times, it is quite understandable and appropriate to be anxious. The goal then is not to try to teach your child never to be anxious. Rather, you can teach your child ways of managing anxiety when that anxiety is excessive and out of proportion to the situation.

Looking at Evidence

The key to changing your thoughts is to really believe the new thoughts, that is, to convince yourself that your original belief is simply not true. We do this by learning to look at the actual evidence. In other words, you need to become a sort of detective or scientist with respect to your life and to look at evidence for every negative thing that you believe. For kids, we talk about *detective thinking,* and in a moment we will be showing you how you can teach your child to think like a detective.

To do detective thinking for yourself, this is what you need to do. Every time you find that you are stressed, anxious, or worried, you need to ask yourself, "What is the negative thing that I am expecting?" or "What do I think is going to go wrong here?" The answer to this question will give you your negative thought or belief. For example, imagine that you have been called into your boss's office and you have no idea why. You find yourself feeling worried. So you could ask yourself, "Why am I worried—what is the negative thing that I am expecting?" Your answer might be, "She is going to criticize me for something I have done wrong." This is your negative belief. Notice that a question such as, "I wonder why she wants to see me?" is not a negative belief and is not what is making you worried. If you come up with an unclear question, you need to keep asking yourself "What *bad thing* am I expecting?"

Once you have identified your negative belief, you need to look at the evidence that either supports or doesn't support it. There will be many types of evidence you can look at, and each thought will require slightly different evidence. However, there are four common types of evidence that we use most often:

1. **Past experience.** One of the easiest sources of evidence is to ask yourself how often you have been in a similar situation and how many of those times it worked out badly. Remember to be very honest with yourself—don't just look at the bad times, but take into account *every* time you have been in a similar situation. For example, you might ask yourself, "How many times in the past has my boss called me in, and how many of those times has it turned out that I did something wrong?"

2. **General information.** You can also often get good evidence by looking at general information relating to a situation or event. This information may take the form of common sense, logic, general knowledge, or even official statistics or research. For example, you might ask yourself, "Do I usually make mistakes that I am unaware of?" or "Is my boss someone who normally criticizes?"

3. **Alternative explanations.** A very useful strategy is to try and think about other possible reasons for the event. The negative interpretation that you had might be one explanation, but are there others? For example, you might consider that your boss has called you in to clarify something she didn't understand, to give you a new task, to ask your opinion on something,

or even to offer you a promotion. None of these is necessarily correct, but it shows you that your negative expectation is only one possibility out of several. Therefore, the negative expectation is not definite and the feared outcome is less likely than you originally thought.

4. **Role reversal.** Finally, a very good source of evidence for some situations, especially interpersonal ones, is to mentally turn the situation around. Pretend that you are the other person and that other person is you or that it is happening to someone else. Then ask yourself how you would feel or what you would think if the situation was reversed. For example, you might ask yourself, "If my colleague had been called in by the boss, would I assume that she would be criticized?" In most cases we are far less negative about other people's lives, and this is a powerful way to realize that you seem to have different expectations for yourself and others.

Looking at all of the evidence in this way can help to convince you that your negative belief ("She is going to criticize me") is just not very likely or is at least not as likely as you originally assumed. But there is one further step to changing your beliefs.

As we said earlier, anxious people tend to overestimate both the likelihood of something bad happening and also how bad it will be. The evidence we have looked at so far should help to reduce the likelihood estimate. But what about the consequences? To examine this, you need to ask yourself one last question—"So what?" In other words, you need to ask yourself, "What would really happen if the bad thing that I am expecting actually did occur?" This question will help you to identify two possible types of answers. One possibility is that you will realize very quickly that the bad thing you were worrying about isn't so bad. The other possibility is that you will come up with another negative belief, and you will then need to look at the evidence for that.

For example, you might ask yourself, "So what if my boss does criticize me about something I did wrong?" One possible answer might be, "I guess it doesn't really matter—I can deal with it." If you *really believe* this, then you should find your worry immediately dropping off. On the other hand, you might come up with a negative consequence such as, "If my boss criticizes my work, she will fire me." In this case, you have now identified another extreme thought and you should go ahead and look at the evidence for this. For example, you might look at the logic of the statement (just because my boss has identified one mistake, does that mean I would get fired?) or at past experience (have you ever been criticized by the boss before and did you lose your job each time?).

Learning to apply realistic thinking to your life is not easy and takes a lot of practice. In reading this section, you may be thinking, "Why are these guys telling me all this—I'm not the one with the problem." This may be true, but the truth is that we can all use realistic thinking at times. We all have times that we get angry, anxious, or stressed when it really isn't necessary. At these times, learning to think more realistically can help to make a difference. But it will only work if you learn it well and really practice at times when you are not too emotional. More importantly, as we said before, you need to learn to do realistic thinking for your child. The best chance your child has for learning to think more realistically is if you and your child's other caregivers can use realistic thinking. This will help your child learn by copying you, and you will also be better able to help your child if you know what you are doing. For these reasons, we strongly urge you to practice realistic thinking right along with your child.

Hopefully, by finding evidence for your own past worry, you can see how analyzing the evidence can help to provide a belief that is more realistic and less likely to cause extreme worry. You may also see how difficult it is to learn this skill at first. The parent activity below will help you to think about evidence for one of your recent worries and will provide you with some questions you can use in future to help you think of evidence. You can then use the Realistic Thinking Worksheet below to do some more practice using realistic thinking on any other worried or other distressing thoughts.

PARENT ACTIVITY: FINDING EVIDENCE FOR MY OWN WORRY

This is by no means an easy skill to learn, for adults or for children. Before you move on to teaching your child about the skill, try it for yourself.

Think of a recent event that caused you worry.

_____

What was your thought or belief about this event?

_____

How worried were you? (Use the worry scale.) _____

What has happened with a similar worry in the past?

_____

_____

What information is available about this event?

_____

_____

What alternative explanations are there?

_____

_____

If you were in another's shoes, what would you believe?

_____

_____

How bad would it be if what you believe did come to pass?

_____

_____

Given all of this evidence, what would have been a realistic belief to hold?

_____

If you had held this belief instead, how worried do you think you would have been? (Use the worry scale.) _____

REALISTIC THINKING WORKSHEET

Event	
Thoughts	
	Worry rating:

Evidence?	
What has happened in the past?	
What do I know about this situation?	
Possible alternative explanations?	
What is most likely to happen?	
What would other people expect?	
How bad would it really be?	

Realistic thought?	
	Worry rating:

TEACHING YOUR CHILD ABOUT REALISTIC THINKING

The points we have been discussing are not easy ones to understand, and it is even harder to apply these principles to your own thoughts and beliefs. It is reasonable to wonder how you are going to teach these ideas to your child. In short, the answer is that you will teach your child a simplified version of these principles. Your child will need to practice using realistic thinking by regularly using a worksheet called the Detective Thinking Worksheet that we will show you later, in the section, "An Example of Detective Thinking," below. This worksheet is very similar to the Realistic Thinking Worksheet that we described above and that hopefully you have tried using. The Detective Thinking Worksheet has slightly easier wording and questions for your child to follow. By using the Realistic Thinking Worksheet for your own worries, you can better understand the process you'll be using with your child.

By the time you have worked through this chapter, your child should have a good understanding of several important points. These points are made in the exercises and readings that you will be working on with your child. However, it is also important that you emphasize and reemphasize these points whenever you can. The key points are these:

- Thoughts are the things that we say to ourselves in our heads.

- Thoughts are important because they cause feelings and behaviors.

- Thoughts can be either calm or worried.

- Worried thoughts can often be changed to calm thoughts by being a good detective and looking for realistic evidence.

The material that you will be working through with your child in this chapter consists of three distinct but related stages, each of which builds upon the stage before. The first stage involves helping your child to understand what thoughts are and to become skilled at identifying his or her own thoughts—you started this in the last chapter. The second stage involves helping your child to understand why thoughts are important, and the third stage involves helping your child to challenge worried thoughts by acting as a detective and examining the evidence. In the following sections, we will include some instructions that you can use to explain these ideas to your child, and at the end of the chapter, we'll offer activities to help your child better understand the ideas.

Why Are Thoughts Important?

At this point you will need to briefly explain the underlying idea of realistic thinking to your child just as we described it at the beginning of this chapter; the children's activities at the end of the chapter will help you with this. Of course, depending on your child's age, this will most likely need to be a more simplified version than was described earlier. It is important to reinforce with your child why thoughts are important, making sure that he or she understands that more than one thought is possible in a situation and that what thought he or she has will determine how he or she feels. The consequence of this is that if children change their thoughts, they can also change how they feel. Activities 11 and 12 will help you to explain these points.

THE DETECTIVE APPROACH

As we discussed earlier, one of the most common mistakes that anxious children make in their thinking is to overestimate the probability that bad or dangerous things will happen to them.*

For this reason, anxious children need to learn to realistically evaluate how likely it is that their negative, anxious interpretations of situations are true or accurate. This will help them to really believe their calm thoughts. In children's terms, we talk about becoming a detective to find clues about whether an anxious thought is true.

In the same way that you have been examining your negative beliefs, your child will need to learn to find evidence about his or her negative expectations. Just as for you, it is important that your child really believes his or her calm thought. For this reason, it is important that you do not simply tell your child that a worried thought is silly or unlikely, as he or she probably won't believe you and it will often upset him or her further. Instead, your child needs to come to the realization, through the process of gathering evidence, that his or her interpretation is unlikely.

In this approach, what children are being asked to do is very similar to the work done by detectives. Both are searching for evidence and clues in order to reach the "truth." To make it more fun, it is a good idea (particularly with younger children) to get them to choose a favorite detective or superhero character (such as Harry Potter, Hermione, Lisa Simpson, Scooby Doo, or Spider-Man). Once children get used to thinking about their favorite detective in this way, you can use this character as a prompt. In other words, when

---

* As you read this section, it is possible that you might think that your child's worries are "real." In other words, perhaps your child is not overestimating. For example, your child's anxieties may be completely focused around real, physical bullying at school, or your child may have a learning disability and be realistically worried about failing school. If this is true for your child, then this approach is not suitable for those specific worries. This program, and realistic thinking in particular, is aimed at managing *excessive* or *unrealistic* anxieties, not fears based on real dangers or difficulties.

your child begins to worry, you simply need to remind him or her to try and think like his or her detective.

The overall approach involves three steps. The first step is for children to work out what they are worried about. They need to identify their worried thought. Remind your child of the difference between thoughts and feelings. It's best if the worried thought is a clear statement of what your child expects to happen. For example, a thought such as, "I am scared that Dad has been killed in a car accident" is a good, clear description that your child can use with his or her detective thinking. In contrast, a thought such as, "I am scared because Dad isn't here" doesn't say what your child is really afraid of and so cannot be worked on easily.

The second step is for your child to gather as many clues as possible about the worried thought. This is where your child gets to play detective and try to work out how he or she might really "know" whether the thing he or she is afraid of will really happen. The easiest types of evidence to find include the following:

- What has happened before in this situation?

- What general things do I know about this situation?

- What else could happen in this situation?

- What is more likely to happen?

- What has happened to other people?

Notice that we don't ask children to think about consequences ("What if it did happen?"). Children, especially younger ones, tend to have a lot of trouble with this. There may be times when you will be able to ask them about possible consequences yourself. But in most cases, it is best to have children focus on evidence to show that what they are scared of probably won't happen.

Finally, based on the evidence children have thought of, they will be in a position to take the third step—to reevaluate their worried thought. Hopefully, they will be able to realize that the worried thought is not actually very likely and that a calm thought is more likely. Remember, this exercise is about *realistic* thinking, not positive thinking. This means that there will be some occasions when the worried thought is actually the more likely one. As an example, think of the child who goes out after dark and finds him or herself in a dark lane and sees someone breaking into a house. It is important to remind children that in such situations, feeling frightened is very natural and useful. The detective thinking that you are teaching your child is designed to help replace worried thoughts with calm thoughts at those times when your child's fears are excessive and unrealistic, not in all situations.

To help you explain the instructions for detective thinking, we have written a possible explanation you could use with your child (see the next section). Go through these instructions with your child together with activity 13, later in the chapter. It is the exceptional child (and parent) who understands the ideas and can use detective thinking right away. You will need to be patient and keep reminding your child of the concepts, making sure he or she does lots and lots of practice. Practice can also be useful for you; we find that many parents have quite a bit of difficulty with this skill. It's not shameful to admit you are having difficulty—don't be afraid to reread the earlier sections and keep practicing.

How to Explain Detective Thinking to Your Child

The children's activities at the end of the chapter will help you to teach your child about detective thinking. The following dialogues and examples will help guide you in how to teach your child this important skill. You can either read the examples to your child or put the information into your own words.

You know now that some thoughts are unhelpful. They make you feel worried and scared; and they can make you do things that lead to bad results for you. Luckily, there are things you can do to beat the worried thoughts.

The first step is to catch them. You've already had some practice at this. Whenever you notice that you are feeling worried or scared or nervous, what you need to do is to catch the worried thought that is causing you to feel this way. Then, write it down on the Detective Thinking Worksheet, next to the "What am I worried about" heading. You can also use the worry scale to write down how bad your worry is.

The next step is to become a detective and hunt down all the clues about your worried thought. A detective's job is to look for evidence and clues so that he or she can find out the truth. This is exactly what you need to do, too. You need to look at your worried thought and ask yourself, "How do I know if it is really true?" Then you need to look for clues to decide whether or not this worried thought is true. Here are some questions you can ask yourself to make sure that you consider all the evidence. (You can point these out to your child on the Detective Thinking Worksheet, or it may be helpful to write these out on cards to help prompt your child while he or she is learning the skill.)

- **What has happened before in this situation?** Have you been in a situation like this before? Did anything bad happen? Did something bad happen every time you were in the situation?

- **What general background information do you know about this situation?** Is this really a bad situation? Have any of your friends or people you know had anything like this happen to them?

- **What else could happen in this situation?** Could there be another reason for this happening? Might something else happen?

Once you have collected your evidence, the last thing you need to do is to think it all through and work out how much you believe in your worried thought (based on the evidence). The question to ask yourself here is, "Based on my clues, what do I really think *will happen? Can I think of a different, calm thought?" Write your calm thought on the last line of the Detective Thinking Worksheet. Finally, you should ask yourself, if I really believe my new calm thought, how worried would I be? Use the worry scale to write down a number.*

An Example of Detective Thinking

The case of the big dog is an example of how Kurt talked with his mother about one of his smaller fears, dogs. You will need to go through lots of practices like this with your child over several weeks to help your child really learn how to use the detective approach. An example of Kurt's Detective Thinking Worksheet appears below. Read through the example below with your child. While you are going through it, look at the Detective Thinking Worksheet to show your child how the various parts were recorded by Kurt and his mother.

KURT'S EXAMPLE: THE CASE OF THE BIG DOG

Mother: I want you to imagine that you are walking down the street one day when a big dog comes running up to you (Kurt's mother writes, "There's a big dog coming toward me" on the "Event" line of the Detective Thinking Worksheet). If you were scared of the dog, what might you think to yourself, Kurt?

Kurt: If it was a really big dog, I would be scared that he was going to bite me.

Mother: Well done Kurt! You've just worked out your worried thought. Let's write that down here (writes, "The dog's going to bite me and I won't be able to stop him" on the "Thoughts" line). Let's look at the worry scale, and you tell me how worried do you think you would be?

Kurt: I think maybe a 7, no, a 9.

Mother:	Okay—we'll write that in here. Now let's pretend that we are detectives and look at the evidence for whether this will or will not happen. What sort of evidence can you think of?
Kurt:	You could run away from the dog.
Mother:	Sure, that's one thing you could do in that situation. Can you think of any evidence for how you know whether the dog will bite you? For example, what has happened before when a dog came running up to you?
Kurt:	I was at my Auntie's house once, and her big black dog Jack came running up to me.
Mother:	What happened when it ran up to you?
Kurt:	Nothing; it was friendly.
Mother:	Good work. So a dog has run up to you before at your Auntie's house, and nothing bad happened. That sounds like an excellent bit of evidence to me. Let's write that down (writes, "A dog has come up to me before, and it didn't bite me" on the "What is the evidence?" line). What did you do when it came over?
Kurt:	Well, I patted it. Its fur was really dirty.
Mother:	Wow, you were so brave that you even patted it. That's fantastic. So, rather than the dog biting you, what could be the other possibility?
Kurt:	It could be friendly, and I could pat it.
Mother:	That's right. Rather than the dog wanting to bite you, the alternative possibility is that it's friendly and wants you to pat it. Do you think this could be a good piece of evidence?
Kurt:	Yes.

Mother:	Yes, I think so too. Good detective work. Let's put the alternative possibility in the evidence section (writes, "The dog is being friendly and wants me to pat him" on the "What is the evidence?" line). I have one more question for you: are all dogs mean, or are lots quite friendly?
Kurt:	Lots are quite friendly.
Mother:	Okay, that's another useful piece of evidence (writes, "Lots of dogs are friendly" on the "What is the evidence?" line). Now that we have looked at some evidence, do you really think that the dog is going to bite you?
Kurt:	I guess not.
Mother:	Good work. From the evidence we came up with, it is probably more likely that it's friendly and that nothing bad will happen. That sounds like a calm thought to me—let's write it here (writes, "The dog is probably friendly, and nothing bad will happen" on the last line).
Mother:	I'm wondering, how would you be feeling if you were thinking that the dog was going to bite you?
Kurt:	Scared.
Mother:	And how would you be feeling if you were thinking that the dog was friendly?
Kurt:	Good.
Mother:	Can you tell me a number for how worried you would be—from your worry scale?
Kurt:	Only a tiny bit—I think a 3.
Mother:	Great work. We can see that the worried thought about the dog would make you feel scared, and this other calm thought would make you feel more happy and relaxed around the dog.

DETECTIVE THINKING WORKSHEET	
Event What is happening?	There's a big dog coming toward me.
Thoughts What am I thinking?	The dog's going to bite me, and I won't be able to stop him. **Worry rating: 9**
What is the evidence? What are the facts? What else could happen? What happened when I worried before? What is likely to happen? What has happened to other people?	A dog has come up to me before, and it didn't bite me. The dog is being friendly and wants me to pat him. Lots of dogs are friendly.
What is my realistic thought?	The dog is probably friendly, and nothing bad will happen. **Worry rating: 3**

Consolidating Detective Thinking

As we have said, detective thinking is going to take a lot of practice before your child (or you) can use it in anxious situations. To help you find evidence for different types of thoughts, we have written a list of questions you can use to gather evidence as well as a series of examples of completed Detective Thinking worksheets. The questions are there to give you some ideas of different ways you can help your child try to come up with evidence. The examples are there for you to read and get a better idea of detective thinking. You might also go through a few of these with your child.

Activities 13 and 14 at the end of the chapter ask your child to apply detective thinking to some smaller practice worries and later to his or her own big worries. Practice task 2 requires your child to practice detective thinking on a day-to-day basis. You should keep practicing detective thinking until your child is able to confidently use this skill without needing your help.

Detective Thinking Questions

Here is a list of many possible questions that you could use to help your child discover evidence. Remember that the questions in the left-most column of the Detective Thinking Worksheet are only prompts. There are many other questions that can be used to find evidence, and for some situations, particular questions would be inappropriate (such as the question, "So what if it did happen?" to a fear about parents dying).

We should also point out here that your child doesn't necessarily have to find lots and lots of evidence or fill the whole page for every worry. Sometimes finding just a single bit of evidence that is really believable is enough to change a worry. The key is to get your child to realize that what he or she is scared will happen, probably won't. Whether this takes lots of little bits of evidence or just a single, key discovery is not important.

SOME USEFUL QUESTIONS

Here is a more detailed list of possible questions that your child might use for various worries.

- What is the evidence that this will not happen?

- What else could happen?

- Are you jumping to a conclusion that this will happen?

- Are your thoughts sensible?

- What is the best or worst that could happen?

- Could you cope if it did happen?

- What is the most likely outcome?

- How will this look in two weeks, a month, or a year's time?

- Are there other explanations for how that other person reacted?

- What are the chances of this happening? (Try a calculation.)

- What has happened in the past?

- What happens to other people in this situation?

- Is this your responsibility?

- Can you really control what will happen?

- Are you underestimating what you can do to deal with this situation?

- Are you being too hard on yourself?

- Are you trying to read someone else's mind?

- If you had a friend in this situation, what would you say to him or her?

SOME SAMPLE DETECTIVE THINKING WORKSHEETS

Here are some Detective Thinking worksheets filled out by the children we introduced in chapter 1. Children often find it much easier to come up with and accept evidence for other people's worries. So you can read over these samples with your child to let him or her see how other children do detective thinking. You could even ask your child to try and think of other evidence that these children might have used.

LASHI'S EXAMPLES

DETECTIVE THINKING WORKSHEET	
Event What is happening?	I am waiting to be picked up from school.
Thoughts What am I thinking?	Mom's been in a car accident. **Worry rating:** 8
What is the evidence?	Mom is only ten minutes late. She could be stuck in traffic or have lost track of time or be stuck on the phone to Nan. Mom has been late to get me twice before; both times she did arrive. There are lots of kids still here; not all their parents could be dead.
What is my realistic thought?	Mom is running late; she will be here soon. **Worry rating:** 3

Event What is happening?	I am spending the day at Grandma's.
Thoughts What am I thinking?	What if Mom gets sick? **Worry rating:** 6
What is the evidence?	Mom was not looking sick when I left. If she did get sick, she is with friends and they will help her. She could be having a great time. Most times when she gets sick, it is only a cold or tummy bug, not something serious. Mom can take care of herself when I'm at school, so why not now?
What is my realistic thought?	Mom is not sick; if she did get sick she could take care of herself. **Worry rating:** 2

KURT'S EXAMPLES

DETECTIVE THINKING WORKSHEET	
Event What is happening?	I just closed the front door.
Thoughts What am I thinking?	My hands are dirty; if I don't wash them, I will get sick. **Worry rating:** 9
What is the evidence?	There is nothing visible on my hands. I have closed a lot of doors in my life and I haven't gotten sick. My body has the antibodies to cope with germs. A lot of very rare things would all have to happen in a row for me to actually get sick. A lot of people don't even bother to wash at all, and they don't get sick.
What is my realistic thought?	My body can cope with a few germs if there were any there to catch. **Worry rating:** 5

Event What is happening?	We are going away for the weekend.
Thoughts What am I thinking?	Something might go wrong. **Worry rating:** 7
What is the evidence?	The weekend is planned out. If something unexpected comes along, it might be a good thing, like a fair. If the car broke down, we could get it fixed and then go home; the worst that could happen would be being bored for a while.
What is my realistic thought?	It is unlikely that something will go wrong, but if it does, I can cope. **Worry rating:** 4

GEORGE'S EXAMPLES

DETECTIVE THINKING WORKSHEET

Event What is happening?	I'm in a class discussion, and everyone has to contribute.
Thoughts What am I thinking?	I'll say something stupid and get laughed at. **Worry rating:** 7
What is the evidence?	I did the reading. I know what the story is about. Most people look very bored already; they probably won't even listen. If they laugh, it could be that I was actually funny. Even if they laugh, in three days they won't remember. I will look even sillier if I don't say anything.
What is my realistic thought?	I know what I am talking about, but most people won't even notice. **Worry rating:** 4

Event What is happening?	I'm being taught a new skill during PE.
Thoughts What am I thinking?	I look like an idiot; I can't do it. **Worry rating:** 10
What is the evidence?	Everyone is learning, and only some seem to be able to do it. The idea is to practice till you get it right. I can usually do new skills okay; I don't need to be perfect at it.
What is my realistic thought?	Just give it a try; that's the only way to learn. **Worry rating:** 5

JESS'S EXAMPLES

DETECTIVE THINKING WORKSHEET	
Event What is happening?	I'm doing math homework and am stuck on question 2.
Thoughts What am I thinking?	I have to answer this question or I'll get in trouble. **Worry rating:** 9
What is the evidence?	I only have to give it a try; I don't have to get it right. I worked out question 1, and this is the same kind of thing. I just have to be patient. If I really can't do it, I won't get in trouble; I just might have to stay in to get some help at recess.
What is my realistic thought?	If I do my best, that's all that will be asked. **Worry rating:** 4

Event What is happening?	I spoke to a new girl in my class.
Thoughts What am I thinking?	My friends won't want to play with me. **Worry rating:** 6
What is the evidence?	I was being polite. She was nice; they might like her too. They may not even know I spoke to her. Sometimes I speak to people that I know they don't like, but they still play with me. I remember they spoke to someone new last term and I still played with them afterward.
What is my realistic thought?	They aren't going to care; they might even be interested in meeting her. **Worry rating:** 1

TALIA'S EXAMPLE

DETECTIVE THINKING WORKSHEET	
Event What is happening?	I was invited to a pool party.
Thoughts What am I thinking?	I can't go if I don't swim. **Worry rating: 6**
What is the evidence?	Not all of the party will be held in the water. I could enjoy the other activities. If I had been sick and wasn't allowed to swim, I could still go. Not everyone likes to swim. If someone asks, I can say that I am not allowed in the water (until I learn to swim, but they don't have to know that).
What is my realistic thought?	I can go to the party and do other things instead of swim. **Worry rating: 1**

A Final Important Comment

You shouldn't be too perfectionistic or allow your child to be perfectionistic while learning these skills. The goal is for your child to learn to replace worried thoughts with realistic, calm ones—and to *believe* them. Exactly how he or she gets to this point is not so important and may vary slightly from child to child. Some children, especially very young ones, may not be able to do the exact sort of evidence collecting that we have suggested here. But they may still begin to think more calmly if they practice coming up with calm, realistic thoughts. For some children who are really having difficulty learning to gather evidence (e.g., for more concrete thinkers), simply learning to identify their own worried thought and then trying to guess a calm thought can still help reduce their anxiety. If your child has really struggled in understanding the detective thinking concepts, you might want to go back to Children's Activity 9 in the last chapter and also to the self-talk activity in this chapter, where a person or two people had different thoughts about the same thing. Then simply go back to getting your child to identify or guess a calm thought for each time he or she gets scared or worried. Using a superhero as a prompt can often be useful—for example, "What would Lisa Simpson think if her mommy was late picking her up from school?" Obviously using the full detective thinking process is usually better. But for some children, simply learning to come up with a calm thought when they feel frightened can help to reduce their fear a little.

Finally, remember that this is not the only technique for overcoming anxiety. If your child really cannot master the detective thinking (after a good and serious try), you might want to move on and rely on some of the other skills that we will cover in the next chapters. We have also included an appendix, at the end of the book, on relaxation. Some children who really can't do detective thinking can become quite good at learning to relax when they get worried. So you might want to consider relaxation as a substitute.

ACTIVITIES TO DO WITH YOUR CHILD ...

CHILDREN'S ACTIVITY 11: WHY ARE THOUGHTS IMPORTANT?

Explain to your child that every situation consists of an event, thoughts, feelings, and behaviors. Emphasize that the same situation can lead to two different thoughts and that the thoughts cause different feelings and behavior. Use the example below or something similar to make this point.

EVENT	THOUGHT	FEELING	BEHAVIOR
Mom is late getting home.	She's been in an accident.	Scared/ worried	I pace up and down the hallway.
	She's stopped to get takeout for dinner.	Happy/ excited	I watch TV while I'm waiting.

Point out that the feeling can be changed by first changing the thought, as the thought comes first. Emphasize that sometimes we have calm thoughts that make us feel good and do helpful things. At other times we have worried thoughts that make us feel bad and do unhelpful things

Read Sam's and Tim's stories and ask your child to identify whose thoughts were helpful and why.

Sam's Story

Sam is at the movie theater with his family. Just before the movie starts, he sees a friend from his class on the other side of the room. Sam waves and calls out to the friend. The friend does not respond. Sam thinks to himself: "He must not have heard me. I'll go over to where he's sitting after the movie has finished and say hello."

Sam feels fine. He sits quietly in his seat and enjoys the movie. When it has finished, he goes over to the other side of the theater where his friend is sitting and says hello. His friend is pleased to see Sam, and they make plans to meet up the next day to play.

Tim's Story

Tim is at the movie theater with his family. Just before the movie starts, he sees a friend from his class on the other side of the room. Tim waves and calls out to the friend. The friend does not respond. Tim thinks to himself: "Oh, he ignored me. He must hate me. Everyone saw that he ignored me. I can't believe what a loser I am."

Tim feels embarrassed and miserable. He doesn't enjoy the movie at all because he's too busy worrying about what happened with his friend. When he sees his friend at school on Monday, Tim avoids him.

CHILDREN'S ACTIVITY 12: SELF-TALK (AMBIGUOUS SITUATIONS)

This activity is designed to help your child better understand the idea that a person can think in different ways in the same situation and that these different thoughts will lead to different feelings and behaviors. Find photos or cartoons of a child in situations such as approaching a big dog, meeting a new child, giving a speech, and waiting for someone to come home (suitable cartoons are included in the workbook). Using the pictures, have your child write two different thoughts that the child in the picture could be having. Encourage your child to identify a calm thought and a worried one.

Then, using a table with the column headings "Thought," "Feeling," and "Behavior," have your child fill in the spaces for a calm response and a worried response for situations such as, "I haven't done my homework," "I want to invite a new friend to my house," "My team has a semifinal tomorrow," and "Summer camp starts on Monday." With each one, point out the way in which it is the thought that changes how you feel and what you decide to do.

CHILDREN'S ACTIVITY 13: DETECTIVE THINKING

For this activity you will need to create your own blank Detective Thinking worksheets based on the earlier examples. You can copy the sample forms that we showed earlier in this chapter or you can use the version provided in the workbook at www.ceh.mq.edu.au/hyac.html. You will need a lot of blank worksheets for this task and for the coming weeks of practice.

Keeping in mind the information you read earlier about teaching detective thinking to your child, explain first that children who worry a lot tend to think that bad things happen a lot or that if a bad thing does happen, it will be a catastrophe, and second, that one way to feel less worried is to work out if the worried thought is realistic. Explain that you can do this by looking for "clues" about whether a worried thought is true or not.

Go through the steps to realistic thinking:

1. Write down the event, thought, and how strong the feeling is on the worry scale.

2. Ask yourself questions (such as, "What are the facts? and "What is likely to happen or has happened before or to other people?) to help find the evidence.

3. List all the things that could happen in the situation.

4. Use the clues to come up with a realistic thought, and rate how worried you would be if you had this thought instead.

Read through one or two of the examples given earlier in the chapter to show your child how detective thinking works.

Teaching your child to use detective thinking is best demonstrated by completing examples. Help him or her to find evidence and realistic thoughts for two simple examples, such as a situation like, "There's a big dog coming toward me" and the subsequent thought, "The dog's going to bite me, and I won't be able to stop him" or the situation, "There's a strange noise outside" and the thought, "A robber is trying to break in."

CHILDREN'S ACTIVITY 14: APPLYING DETECTIVE THINKING TO BIG WORRIES

This activity should be done *after* your child has had at least one week of consistent practice of doing detective thinking on his or her smaller worries. Once your child starts to understand the process, have him or her complete Detective Thinking worksheets for bigger worries, trying to cover at least two situations. Remember to use the questions listed earlier to help your child gather the best evidence for each situation. If your child is having trouble, let him or her "coach" you on one of your own worries. Get your child to ask you the questions and help you come up with evidence for the worry, and then help you come up with a calm, realistic thought. It is often easier to practice when the situation is not personal.

In particular, encourage your child to come up with a lot of evidence for these big worries. The more evidence your child finds, the more likely it is that he or she will find a realistic thought to believe.

CHILDREN'S PRACTICE TASK 2: DETECTIVE THINKING

Detective thinking is not an easy skill to learn. The key is practice. Detective thinking will continue for the rest of the program. Children should fill in a Detective Thinking Worksheet every time they feel at all nervous, shy, worried, or frightened. The more that children practice, the better they will get at it, and the more likely they will be to use detective thinking when they're actually feeling anxious. To begin, you'll probably need to be quite involved and help your child considerably. As he or she gets better, you should help less and less. Older children might pick up the skills in a few days while younger children may need help for many weeks. But remember, this isn't a race—each child needs to take whatever time is needed to master the skill.

Each afternoon or evening you should sit down with your child and think through the day and go over detective thinking for any bad experiences or remembered worries. Even doing them after the fact is good practice. Obviously, the key is for your child to be able to use detective thinking when in a frightening situation. Therefore, whenever you notice your child getting nervous, try to prompt him or her to use this skill. Early on in the process, you will need to prompt in detail, helping your child with the exact steps and questions; obviously this means that you will need to commit this process and the evidence-gathering questions to memory. As your child gets better at the skill, prompts may simply take the form of reminders such as, "What would a detective think in this situation?"

CHAPTER HIGHLIGHTS

In this chapter, you and your child learned . . .

- In any situation, it is possible to have more than one thought about what is happening.

- Thoughts can lead to different feelings such as feeling calm or worried.

- Worried thoughts are often unrealistic, but by being a detective, a person can find evidence to help discover a more realistic thought.

- The process of realistic thinking, also called detective thinking, involves the following actions:

  - Identifying the worried thoughts in your head

  - Using questions to help find evidence that suggests that the worried thought is not true

  - Using the evidence to create a calm thought

  - A calm thought can help you to feel less worried.

Your child will need to do the following:

- Complete the children's activities with the help of a parent or other adult.

- Practice detective thinking as often as possible. The more your child can do it, the better he or she will get at it—but it needs to be done at least once per day. Detective thinking and filling out Detective Thinking worksheets will need to continue for at least the next two to three weeks, but probably quite a bit longer.

CHAPTER 4

Parenting an Anxious Child

YOUR CURRENT STRATEGIES

There are many different ways of handling a child's anxiety. Some of the more common strategies include reassuring a child (for example, repeatedly telling the child that "everything will be all right"), telling a child exactly how to handle the situation, empathizing with a child's anxiety by discussing in detail what makes you anxious and afraid, being tough with a child and not letting him or her avoid the situation, removing a child from the feared situation, allowing a child to avoid the situation, prompting a child to independently decide how to cope constructively with his or her anxiety, ignoring a child's anxiety, and becoming impatient with a child. You probably find that you use several of these strategies at different times with differing rates of success. As a general rule, some of these strategies are effective in managing child anxiety and some of them are not. Each strategy will be reviewed in more detail

PARENT ACTIVITY: WHAT ARE MY CURRENT STRATEGIES?

Listed below are some of the common ways that parents react to their child's anxiety. Thinking about your own parenting strategies, comment on how useful or successful each is with your child. You can add your own strategies to this list as well.

Strategy	Successful or useful?
Providing reassurance	
Telling child what to do	
Empathizing	
Being tough	
Allowing avoidance	
Prompting independence	
Ignoring	
Becoming impatient	

In case you're beginning to wonder whether the way in which you parent your child is going to be called into question, rest assured—it's not! The above list has been generated with the help of other parents who have been involved with this program in the past. It's not meant to gauge how "good" a parent you are. Rather, it is intended to show that lots of other parents face similar difficulties and often respond to them in similar ways.

Being the parent of an anxious child can be really tough, and no doubt there are times when you feel that you just don't know what to do or say in response to your child's anxiety. There are probably many times when you feel that nothing that you do or say seems to work. When a person is really caught up in a situation or problem, it's very difficult for that person to view the situation objectively.

There is no right or wrong way of handling a child, and each child and each family is different. However, there are some things that parents can do to reduce the anxiety that their child will experience in the long run, while on the other hand, sometimes parents and children slip into a pattern that isn't very helpful for addressing a child's anxiety. Hopefully, this chapter will help you gain some objectivity in thinking about the strategies that you are currently using to handle your child's anxiety. By carefully considering the advantages and disadvantages associated with each strategy, you will be able to make informed decisions regarding whether or not a certain strategy is likely to be effective in the long term with your child.

UNHELPFUL WAYS OF DEALING WITH ANXIETY IN CHILDREN

While it is true that there are no wrong ways to handle a child, sometimes parents might react to their child's anxiety in ways that help to keep the anxiety going or even to increase it in the longer term.

Excessively Reassuring Your Child

Based on parents' reports, this strategy appears to be very commonly used with anxious children. Examples of ways in which parents attempt to reassure their children include physical affection or closeness or telling the child that "everything will be all right" and that "there is nothing to be afraid of." Within reason, these are all great strategies, and if they feel right for you, you should continue to use them to some degree. It is only when you find yourself constantly having to reassure your child that alarm bells might start ringing. Loving your children and giving them comfort, security, and reassurance when they are hurt is an important part of parenting. We would never say that you should not reassure your child. In fact, too little reassurance can be as bad as too much. Children who never get reassurance or comfort from their parents are likely to feel insecure and alone. But because of their personalities, anxious children are often not able to rely on themselves and will ask for reassurance far more than other children. That's when you can start to get into a vicious circle.

Reassurance is a natural parental response to a child's distress. Unfortunately, to an anxious child, reassurance is like water off a duck's back: it has very little effect. More importantly, even if reassurance might help to relieve your child's anxiety a little in the short run, in the long run, the more reassurance you give as a parent, the more reassurance your child will demand.

What is really important is to think about *when* you give your child lots of attention and reassurance. Obviously, when a child is really hurt or has gotten a fright from a potentially serious situation, then you cannot give too much love and attention. Let's say your child was crossing the road and a car screeched to a stop only inches from your child's terrified face. There is no way that you could give too many hugs and kisses in a situation like this. But when your child begins to get scared at times when the fear is excessive, then your hugs and kisses simply give your child the message that there really is something awful there to worry about. Let's say your child starts to cry when you want to go out for the evening and a sitter arrives.

Leaping in and showering your child with hugs and kisses only gives the message, "This really is an awful situation."

Reassurance is a form of positive attention for your child. This means that every time your child gets anxious and you reassure him or her, you are actually rewarding your child's anxiety. In some cases, this might make the anxiety seem almost worthwhile for the child. At the very least, it can help to teach children that they cannot cope by themselves and that they need you to handle difficult situations. For this reason, you may find that for your anxious child, you will actually need to hold off your reassurance even more than you would for a nonanxious child simply so that your anxious child is forced to learn that he or she can do things for him- or herself.

So what do you do when your child does seek help or reassurance? The best strategy is to help teach children how they can come up with answers themselves rather than always expecting you to do it for them. There are two common ways of doing this. One way is described in detail later in this chapter (see "Helpful Ways of Dealing with Anxiety in Children"). Another, is to prompt your child to use detective thinking. In other words, rather than simply giving your child reassurance (e.g., "Don't worry; it will be all right"), it would be much better to get your child to apply his or her own detective thinking to the worry.

When you are dealing with a child who has become used to asking for reassurance a great deal, you may need to begin gradually to give less and less help over time. For example, if you decide to encourage your child to use his or her own detective thinking rather than coming to you for reassurance, you may need to spend a little time with your child going through detective thinking the first few times. After a short while, you can gradually expect your child to do more and more of the detective thinking independently. Eventually, if your child comes to you seeking reassurance, you should be able simply to tell him or her to do his or her own detective thinking about the problem.

If you are going to make a change from always helping your child as much as he or she wants, to withdrawing a little, it is very important that you let your child know. A sudden change without explanation might leave your child feeling hurt, unloved, and afraid. No matter how young your child is, you should explain clearly what the changes are going to be and why you are making them. It's also a very good idea to introduce rewards (and of course lots of praise) when your child successfully solves a problem by him- or herself. Finally, it is absolutely essential that you and other adults in your child's life are consistent. No matter how hard it is, it is important not to give in to your child's requests for reassurance (within reason). Don't enter into extended arguments with children. Rather, inform them clearly and calmly that you are confident that they know the answer and you are not going to discuss it any more. Then ignore any further requests for reassurance. Don't forget to reward and praise your child for successful self-reliance (i.e., for not seeking reassurance).

As you will see in the following example, for Kurt and his mother, this process does require that parents keep to their decision despite their child asking the questions. Children learn that persistence often pays off, so as a parent, you will need to outlast their persistence and stick to your plans.

KURT'S EXAMPLE

Whenever they're going on a family outing, Kurt bugs his parents with repeated questions about what will happen, who will be there, what they should take, what he should wear, and so on. In the past, Kurt's parents have tried everything to get him to relax and ask fewer questions. Usually, however, they end up answering his questions for a while, eventually losing patience and yelling at him. Finally, Kurt's mother decided that it was time to tackle this problem in a different way (his father was not very interested in the program).

To begin, Kurt's mother sat down with him at a calm time to discuss the issue. She told him that she loved his usual questions and his curiosity but that when he was worried about things, he would often begin to ask too many nagging questions. She explained that she knew he was very smart and that he was now old enough to answer many of his own questions. She said that the next time he began to worry and ask too many questions, she would help him to do his detective thinking to try to come up with his own answers. After that, Kurt's mother explained that she and his father would ignore any further "worry questions." They would be very pleased with him if he could do his own detective thinking and not ask them any worry questions.

A week later, Kurt's family was invited to a friend's house for lunch. As the time approached, Kurt began with some questions. He was particularly worried about whether he would know anyone and about the possibility that the other kids might not like him. As soon as he began to ask questions, his mother sat down with him and went through his detective thinking with him. She encouraged him to think about how many times he had previously been to visit family friends and had known people, whether other kids usually found him likeable, what he was likely to think (based on previous experience) of the other children there, and so on. After Kurt had been through the evidence, his mother praised him and went about her work. The next time that Kurt asked a question about the visit, she said to him, "You know that we have already talked about this and done the detective thinking. You know that you have the answers and that you don't need me to tell you. If you ask again, I am not going to answer you, but I am very happy to talk about anything else you would like to discuss." When Kurt asked again, his mother simply ignored the question. When he did not ask any questions for ten minutes, she said, "Kurt, do you realize that you haven't asked me anything about our outing today for the last ten minutes? I'm really proud of how brave you are being. Keep up the good work." Kurt asked no more questions about the visit that day. After the visit, Kurt's parents let him stay up a little later to watch a movie he had been excited about.

Being Too Involved and Directive

When a child is extremely anxious, some parents will try to take over and direct their child. In other words, they will tell the child exactly what to do, how to behave, and what to say in the anxiety-provoking situation or they will do things on behalf of their child.

GEORGE'S EXAMPLE

Take George's parents for instance. George becomes very anxious when in social situations with other children. On one particular occasion, George and his father went to the birthday party of a younger cousin. George spent most of the time sitting beside his father and not mixing with the other children. At one point, a clown arrived and began handing out candy. George's father could see that George would have loved to have some candy but that he was not going to step forward and ask for any because he was too shy. So his father leapt up and went to the clown to get some candy for George. George blushed from ear to ear but was very pleased with the candy.

The manner in which parents sometimes take over for their anxious children is an excellent example of what we call a *vicious circle*. Usually, parents only adopt this strategy after the repeated experience of watching their child feel helpless with anxiety. Most parents don't tell their kids what to do in anxiety-provoking situations out of natural bossiness. Rather, parents behave in this way because they feel so much for their child when they see the child become gripped by fear. In the short term, this strategy of stepping in helps to reduce the children's fear and gets them what they want. However, if you think about it, this reliance on parental direction is actually a form of avoidance. In the above example, George has learned that he is unable to handle the feared situation himself and that he can only do it with his father's help. In the long term, this helps to further reduce his self-confidence and to keep his anxiety going.

Even though it can be very painful, it is vitally important that you do not do too much for your child. The bottom line is that children often learn best by being allowed to make their own mistakes. Also, children can only learn that situations are not dangerous, and that they can cope, if they are forced to experience the situation. We will discuss this principle in much more detail in the coming chapters. For now, it's important for you simply to think about whether you sometimes become too involved with your child's activities or take things over for him or her.

So how much involvement is "too much"? Unfortunately, there's no simple answer to this question. There is no way to quantify how involved to be, and, of course, every parent and child and situation will be different. What you need to ask yourself is whether you think that you help your child more than other parents do and whether your child relies on him- or herself less than other children his or her age. You may need to think about concrete examples of times when your child has appeared helpless and you felt you had to step in. Talk to other parents and ask what they or their child would do in such situations. And above all, ask yourself, "Did I *really need* to step in? What would have been the worst thing to happen, if I hadn't?" As we said earlier, with an anxious child, it's possible that you might need to help even less often than you would with a less-anxious child.

Permitting Avoidance

Anxious children try to avoid lots of activities. As a parent, it is hard to continually push your child to face fears, so sometimes, you might give in and let your child avoid them. If this happens occasionally, it's understandable. Obviously, in the short run, your child's anxiety and distress will drop, and you will also make yourself very popular by allowing your child to get out of doing things that he or she does not want to do. However, if it becomes a common habit, the long-term consequences of permitting avoidance in your child are very serious. As long as children continue to avoid, they will not overcome their anxiety. At this point, you don't need to do anything about avoidance, aside from be aware of it. We will discuss how to deal with avoidance in chapter 5.

JESS'S EXAMPLE

Jess's worries get much worse whenever there is a new or rare activity that she is meant to participate in. Jess's parents know that events like the school athletics day or family outings with her cousins will cause several sleepless nights and a lot of tears. It has been this way for a very long time. When there is no other choice, Jess is made to go to these events, but her parents often let her stay home or they decline the invitations themselves whenever possible as it is all too hard. Jess has not gone to athletics days for the last two years, and last Christmas, Jess, her siblings, and parents did not attend the family Christmas party because it was being held at her aunt's place rather than her grandparents' house where it had been in previous years. Sometimes Jess's parents try to get around this problem by not telling her about events until they are in the car and on their way; for example, they might use this strategy when visiting the dentist. This often backfires; Jess becomes panicky, and they have to turn back anyway.

Jess knows she does not have to do activities that worry her a lot and will now just say to her parents, "I just don't think I can do that." Consequently she is missing out on many enjoyable activities, as well as ones that are necessary for her education and health.

Becoming Impatient with Your Child

Unfortunately, as many parents tell us, it's all too easy to become impatient and frustrated with an anxious child. Nothing you do or say seems to help. At times, it can feel as though children are deliberately clinging to their anxiety. Often it feels like, "They could do it if only they would try harder." While it's understandable that you might sometimes lose your patience, obviously becoming angry with your child will only serve to make him or her more frightened and dependent. If you feel yourself losing patience, it is helpful to ask another person (such as your partner) to help, or to leave the situation for a short while to gather your thoughts. It can sometimes be useful to try and remind yourself what you are asking your child to do. Imagine having to confront something really terrifying (like walking into a biker's party and asking them to turn the music down) and you might be able to understand the difficulty that your child has to face.

LASHI'S EXAMPLE

Lashi's dad came to pick her up on Friday afternoon for an overnight visit. Lashi's mom had plans to go out with her best friend to a movie while Lashi was away; she hadn't been to a movie in eighteen months and was really looking forward to it. Lashi had been worried about visiting her dad all week. She thought that her mom would have a terrible accident while she was not there and that her mom would die because no one would be able to call for help. She had discussed this with her mom at length, and they had made an agreement that after the movie, Lashi's mom would call her to say goodnight.

Before school on Friday, Lashi dragged her feet a lot and would not help to get her bag ready to take for the night. Her mom didn't want to rock the boat, so, although she yelled several times in frustration, she sent Lashi to school and got the bag ready herself. When the afternoon came and Lashi's dad arrived, Lashi became distraught. She clung to her mother and was shouting and screaming in the front yard. Lashi's mom lost her temper, smacked Lashi twice, and put her into the car so her dad could quickly drive off.

Lashi's mom felt awful. She knew Lashi was scared but she had just had enough. She didn't end up enjoying the movie, and when she called Lashi afterward, even though she had settled pretty well, Lashi's mom offered to pick her up and bring her home. Lashi jumped at the chance and came home, and her mom then spent extra time with her to make up for losing her temper.

PARENT ACTIVITY: ANALYZING UNHELPFUL STRATEGIES

To help become aware of the "traps" that you are currently falling into, complete the following table. Think about the times that you use these strategies. Record which of your child's worries typically prompts you to use the strategy and what the problem is with that, that is, what is your child learning when you do this?

Strategy	What worry prompts this strategy?	What is your child learning?
Excessive reassurance		
Being too directive		
Permitting or encouraging avoidance		
Becoming impatient		

HELPFUL WAYS OF DEALING WITH ANXIETY IN CHILDREN

While there is no single way to handle a child's fears, and everyone will have their own ways of doing things, there are ways that parents can act that will help their child to learn that "Nothing bad will happen" and "I can handle it."

Rewarding Brave, Nonanxious Behavior

All children, no matter how anxious, will at certain times do things that are frightening for them. As a parent, you should look out for any examples of this type of bravery, no matter how small, and reward your child for them. This will make it more likely that the bravery will happen again. Think of it as fanning the small embers of a fire to get it to grow. At first, you need to look for any example of bravery and make a big fuss over it. Later, as your child becomes less anxious, you can reward only the more obvious examples. Make sure you don't set your expectations too high. Remember, what may seem like a small thing to you may be extremely difficult for a nervous child. You will need to make sure you look for behaviors that are brave based on your child's personality, not on anyone else's standards. By pointing to and focusing on successes, you will help your child to build self-confidence as well as help your child realize what he or she is capable of.

In addition to looking for naturally occurring bravery, at times you may want to encourage your child to do things that are a little challenging for him or her. Again, this needs to be rewarded. We will discuss this strategy in more detail later in the program.

Rewards can fall into two broad types—material and nonmaterial. Material rewards are the ones most of us think of immediately. These might include money, food, stickers, or toys. The child is given the reward, say, a small toy, after the brave action is noticed. Nonmaterial rewards include praise, attention, and interest from the parent. Parental attention is an extremely powerful reward. Most children, especially younger ones, will do almost anything for the approval and praise of their parents. Spending extra time with children (e.g., playing a game or going for a bike ride) is a great way to reward them for brave, nonanxious behavior. Whenever possible, we suggest you use nonmaterial rewards because they have the added benefit of giving your child a sense of security and self-esteem.

It is also important to keep your rewards varied. If your child keeps getting the same reward over and over, that reward will very quickly lose its impact. There are several points to remember when using rewards:

- In order to be effective, rewards must be meaningful to the child. There is no point in rewarding a child with something he or she doesn't like. The easiest way to make sure that the child will work for a reward is to discuss it. Find out what he or she wants most at this moment.

- Discuss clearly with your child exactly what he or she needs to do to get rewards. There is no point showering rewards on children if they think the rewards came for no reason. It is important that the child knows exactly why he or she is getting the reward and how it could be gotten again. Praise should be clear and specific. You want your child to know exactly what he or she has just done that you liked and want him or her to repeat in the future. For example, saying, "David, you were able to go by yourself with Mrs. Jones into class this morning instead of needing me to come in with you. I was really proud of you" is much more useful than saying, "You were a good boy today, David."

- The rewards must be in keeping with the activity, and you need to make sure that you give the child a reward that is the right size for the difficulty of the activity. For example, if your child is terrified of dogs and has just spent the last half hour with the neighbor's dog, which he or she has never approached before, it is not fair to give only a small token or two minutes of your time. On the other hand, if your child has done something that was only slightly difficult, you are leaving yourself with nowhere to go if you reward him or her with a new television.

■ Most importantly, rewards must be given as soon as possible after the brave action has occurred and they must be delivered if promised. Consistency is essential for effective parenting. Children will learn very quickly to stop trusting a parent's word if they find that promises are not delivered. *If you promise your child a reward, it must be delivered.* Similarly, rewards lose their effectiveness the greater the time between the event and the reward. If your child does something brave on Monday and you give a small reward the following Saturday, the whole impact will have been lost. For maximum impact, the reward should be delivered immediately. That is why your own time and attention can be so much better than buying a gift. Of course, there will be times when delivering an immediate reward is just not practical. For example, you may decide to reward your child by going skiing together. Obviously, this can't be done immediately and may need to wait until the weekend. In this case, it is useful to give some sort of interim reward. For example, you may make up a small voucher that clearly says the reason for earning the voucher on it, and your child can exchange it during the weekend for the ski trip. At the very least, if the reward is delayed, you need to make an immediate fuss and give attention to the brave act and make it very clear that the later reward and the brave act are connected.

■ If you have other children, you may find that they become resentful of the extra attention and rewards that your anxious child is getting. One way around this might be to introduce a reward system for all children in the family. You can introduce a chart where each child can earn rewards, although the rewards might be earned by different behaviors for each child. In this way, you can build bravery in all your children if needed, or you could use the rewards for your other children to increase helpful habits such as obedience, brushing teeth, tidying their rooms, and so on. If they are older (mature) siblings, explain to them that their little brother or sister is doing some extra hard work to overcome his or her fears and that this is something that they would not normally be expected to do, so it deserves extra rewards. If they want to earn rewards too, they have to work on something equally as difficult or unusual (like doing an extra half-hour of music practice each day or learning how to touch-type).

TEACHING YOUR CHILD ABOUT REWARDS

In the same way that we emphasize rewards as an important part of parenting management, we believe it is also important for children to learn what rewards are and about self-rewarding. Although most children have no trouble telling you what things they would like to receive as rewards, they generally only think of rewards as big and small material items, not as the wide range of items that are actually possible. There are two purposes here: first, to get an idea of what rewards your child would like to earn throughout the program (remember rewards must be meaningful to your child, not you) and second, to get your child to begin to reward him- or herself for the efforts made. In this chapter's activities, your child will be learning to identify rewards and to self-reward.

Ignoring Behaviors That You Don't Want

This is really the flip side of the previous strategy. It involves removing your attention from your child's anxious behavior and attending again (and praising) when the anxious behavior has stopped. The idea is that when you notice a behavior that you are not happy with (for example, your child repeatedly complaining about feeling sick before school), you need to stop any interaction with your child as long as he or she is doing that behavior (complaining). Of course, it is essential that your child understand exactly why you are ignoring him or her and exactly what he or she needs to do in order to regain your attention. Using this strategy should be immediately followed by specific praise for something good that the child is doing (e.g., complaining stops for one minute). Ignoring is a particularly useful strategy for dealing with reassurance seeking (as we discussed above in the section "Excessively Reassuring Your Child"). This strategy must always be used carefully and only in relation to a specific behavior. It's important that your child understands that it is the particular behavior in which he or she is engaging that is unacceptable to you and not his or her general character. In addition, as we discussed earlier, it is important to remove your attention from your child's reassurance seeking in a gradual and systematic way and to encourage children to use a strategy where they can do it themselves (such as their detective thinking).

KURT'S EXAMPLE

All the way to school each day, Kurt used to ask his dad whether he had fed the dog, put her outside, and filled up her water bowl, even though he had never forgotten to do these things before. His dad made an agreement with Kurt that he would no longer answer these questions but would instead start singing along with the radio. He reminded Kurt that he was perfectly capable of remembering, himself, whether those things had been done and also reminded Kurt of the evidence that he had never forgotten these things before. The next day when Kurt asked the questions, his dad said, "I don't answer those questions anymore—try and think of the evidence yourself"; he then turned on the radio and started singing. Kurt looked annoyed, even got mad one morning, but after a week, he no longer asked the questions and soon stopped worrying about these things.

Prompting Your Child to Cope Constructively

When you are talking with your child about the things that make him or her anxious, it's important that you express your empathy and understanding in a calm and relaxed manner. Children need to feel listened to, understood, and supported, but it is equally important that they are encouraged to constructively solve the problem of their anxiety rather than focusing on how bad they feel. A stepped problem-solving approach will be introduced later in the chapter as a way of handling anxious moments.

Parents who use this strategy typically prompt their children to think for themselves about how to constructively handle an anxiety-provoking situation. This is quite different from parents who tell their children exactly what to do in the anxiety-provoking situation.

GEORGE'S EXAMPLE

George is highly anxious about a debate that he has to take part in at school. He is very upset and imagines the worst possible outcome. George is sure that he will make a mess of his speech and look like a complete idiot. He complains that he has a headache and that his stomach hurts.

George's mom comes and sits down with him. She says to him, "George, I can understand that you feel worried about the debate. But the fact is that you have to do it for class, and at the moment, you're just not helping yourself. You're saying a lot of negative things about how things are going to go, and that must be making you feel worse. Plus, you're talking yourself into feeling sick. What you're doing right now isn't making you feel any better, is it?" George agrees with his mother. She then goes on, "Okay, so what can you do that might help? What can you do that would make you feel better?" George answers this by saying that staying away from school on the day of his team's debate would help him feel better. His mom points out that George's teacher would probably just postpone his team's debate until he came back to school and she also says that George will have to do more public speaking tasks now that he is in high school; if he puts it off now, the next time will be even harder. George can see the logic of this, especially the first point. He suggests that maybe if he practiced the speech with his mom, he might feel better about it. She praises him for coming up with a constructive way of dealing with his anxiety and agrees to practice with him.

In this example, George's mom is prompting George to come up with his own solutions. She is not encouraging him to rely on her because she is not directly intervening. Instead, she is encouraging him to take responsibility for managing his own anxiety in a constructive manner. At the same time, she is firmly not allowing him to avoid the debate.

Encouraging your child to use the detective approach to evaluate the realistic probability of his or her negative, worrying thoughts being true is an important component of this strategy. Prompting your child to independently decide how to cope constructively with anxiety is a good long-term strategy, because it involves showing faith in your child's abilities. You would be surprised at how often children are able to rise to meet their parents' expectations. If you believe that your child possesses the ability to overcome challenges and to solve problems, he or she is more likely to believe this too.

Modeling Brave, Nonanxious Behavior

Children learn how to behave by observing others, and most significantly, their parents, especially when children are younger. Thus, as a parent, everything that you do or say has added significance because you are serving as a model for your child. And who do you think your child is likely to most closely relate to with respect to his or her anxiety—the calm, relaxed one in the family or the slightly nervous, worried one? Naturally, when it comes to their fears and worries, anxious children will most strongly relate to a parent who, like them, might also seem to have a few fears of his or her own. So if one or both parents can think of a few of their own fears and worries, then parents have the power to really help their child cope with anxiety.

The very best type of model is a *coping model,* that is, a model who can show that he or she experiences fears and worries and also can show how to cope constructively with these difficulties. This type of model is much more effective than one who never seems to have any difficulties. So if you fit the bill, it is really important that you don't try and hide your fears from your child or pretend that you never get scared. All this does is show your child that it is embarrassing or "weird" to be scared. Instead, you need to see managing your fears and worries as a shared activity—something you and your child can work on together.

Once you start talking openly with your child about your own fears, you can begin to use yourself as a model or practice example for your child. For example, you can ask your child to help you with your detective thinking. Children will love this, and it will help them to really understand how they can think more realistically. Later, when we start to work on building stepladders (see chapter 5), you and your child can each have your own stepladders and can use this to make anxiety management more fun. For example, your child can help you work on your stepladder and approach your fears, which will help him or her understand more about overcoming fears. Or you could set up a challenge where you see who can work his or her way up a stepladder first.

Of course for some parents of anxious children, the parent's own anxiety can actually be a serious problem. If you believe that you have a problem with anxiety and are having trouble handling it yourself, it is important for you to see a mental health professional so that you can begin to model more effective coping for your child.

TALIA'S EXAMPLE

Talia was beginning to prepare to face her fear of water. One day when her grandma was over, Talia found out that her grandma was also scared of water and that she had never learned to swim. They talked for a while about the things that her grandma had missed out on because she didn't know how to swim. Together they decided they could both face their fear of water and learn how to swim. They booked swimming lessons for each other and made a pact to have learned to swim twenty-five meters by Christmas when they would go swimming together. Even though Talia didn't live near her grandma, they kept each other up to date on their progress by phone. Talia felt confident that if her grandma could do it, so could she.

PARENT ACTIVITY:
ANALYZING HELPFUL STRATEGIES

In this activity, you need to think through how you might apply the helpful strategies. Keep in mind both your child's most common worries and how you might overcome the unhelpful strategies that you analyzed in the last activity.

Strategy	What worries or behaviors could I use this strategy on?	How might I do this?
Rewarding brave, nonanxious behavior		
Ignoring behavior I don't want		
Prompting constructive coping		
Modeling brave, nonanxious behavior		

IMPORTANT PRINCIPLES TO REMEMBER WHEN DEALING WITH CHILDREN

There are a number of common difficulties for parents in successfully managing their child's behavior. Although some of these principles may seem obvious, they are easy to forget.

Being Consistent

It is important that you try to reward (or punish) your child consistently. Children need to learn that certain behaviors lead to desirable consequences and that others lead to undesirable consequences. In this way you can encourage your child to behave appropriately. You need to discuss this with your partner and decide on a joint strategy. Similarly, your parenting will work best if everyone who is involved with raising that child is also on board, including step-parents, grandparents, and so on. Naturally this will not always be possible, and this is when things might start to get difficult. But the more you can have consistent rules and consequences for your child, the better your child will be at learning to manage his or her behavior.

Keeping Your Emotions in Check

At times, all children can be very frustrating and worrying! This is especially true for anxious children. What could be more frustrating than running late to get out the door when your child is refusing to get dressed because he or she is scared to go into the other room alone? As understandable as it is to get mad, you need to remember that you become far less effective as a coach when you are very emotional (e.g., angry or anxious) because at such times it is harder to be consistent. Plan ahead for ways in which you can give yourself a "time-out" from interactions with your child when those interactions provoke strong emotional responses in you. When you take time away, tell your child what you are doing and let him or her know that you will come back a little later. Similarly when you work on your child's anxiety program, it is important to do so at a pre-planned time when you are both calm and relaxed. You should not be trying to teach your child new lessons on the run when he or she is crying with fear at going out the door. Finally, when you do find yourselves escalating, try to get away and gather your thoughts. Try to get a partner, friend, or older sibling to stay with your child and try to explain that you need to get away to calm down. Then go into another room and try to get your thoughts together. You'll be able to deal with your child's anxiety far more effectively when you are keeping your cool.

Distinguishing Between Anxious and Naughty Behavior

One of the most common difficulties parents have is drawing a line between a child's anxious behaviors and times when a child is just being naughty. Parents are also often getting a mixture of advice from well-meaning others who believe that all of the child's behaviors are pure naughtiness and should therefore be punished. Unfortunately the two behaviors can look very similar, but the anxious ones don't deserve to be punished, making it difficult for parents to know what to do. Another difficulty can be that some anxious children would much rather get in trouble than face a feared situation (the type of trouble a child will get in is usually pretty predictable and therefore quite safe), so they will deliberately mess up to get out of it.

There are three principles that can help you to distinguish between anxious behaviors and naughty behavior:

1. Even if a child is anxious at the time, any form of verbal or physical aggression is not acceptable. That means that swearing, calling people names, hitting, and throwing things should all lead to immediate consequences. In the real world, these behaviors are not excused just because someone is feeling bad, therefore allowing children to act like this without consequences will in the long run disadvantage them. They need to learn to deal with their emotions appropriately, even when these feelings are really strong.

2. You need to look at the situation in detail to see if there is a reason why your child might be avoiding a task. For example, if you have asked your child to go and brush his or her teeth and this hasn't happened, stand back and look at the situation. Suppose that you know that your child is scared of the dark and the bathroom is at the end of the hallway and at the moment there are no lights on. In that case, it is quite possible that your child is avoiding the task rather than being disobedient. However, if there are no such limitations and your child is just glued to the television, then it is probably disobedience and turning off the television immediately for ten minutes would be an appropriate response.

3. You can also look at how consistently your child seems to avoid a situation. For example, if your child says he or she is too scared to go into his or her room every time there is homework to do but seems quite happy to sit in there for hours at the computer, then you may assume that your child is exaggerating his or her fears.

Children who get out of activities by complaining that they are afraid, often do look quite happy when they succeed, that is, do not have to do the task. This can fool people into thinking that this is just manipulative behavior. However, it is important to look at what you know of your child's fears and worries and see if this behavior makes sense from that point of view. If you worried about that thing, would you be willing to do the task? If the answer is no, it points to an area where you need to apply anxiety management skills. If the task is not associated with a known fear, then it is probably safe to insist that your child complete the task without working on the anxiety.

Managing Naughty Behavior

Although this is not a course that will help you deal with deliberate naughtiness or disobedience, we encourage the use of nonphysical punishment when a child's behavior gets out of hand. Again, these punishments need to be used consistently and with emotions in check.

TIME-OUT

This is a very useful form of "punishment," especially for younger children. Before using time-out, the terms need to be carefully discussed, that is, why a time-out is necessary, what behavior will result in a time-out, where the time-out will be (choose a boring place like the bathroom or an entryway), how long your child must stay in time-out (generally five to fifteen minutes for primary school children), how he or she must behave while in time-out (the time doesn't start until your child is quiet), and what you want to see at the end of a time-out (completion of a task, an apology). You and your child should also agree on what will happen if he or she does not adhere to the time-out agreement (e.g., loss of a privilege until the time-out is completed).

As an example, it may be that you and your child agree to use a time-out when your child starts shouting. If he or she shouts, the time-out is five minutes in the bathroom. The time does not start until your child is quiet. After five minutes of time-out, the child can come back to the conversation and explain (in a reasonable tone) what he or she is upset about. After using time-out, parents should find the next opportunity to praise their child for good behavior—in the example above, the parent would praise the child the next time that the child talks calmly.

JESS'S EXAMPLE

Jess has recently been aggressive when she becomes highly anxious. She will yell that she hates people and has hit both her mom, Maggie, and her dad, Dan, several times when they have tried to insist that she complete a task. Her parents are at a bit of a loss as to what to do with her when she is like this but have tended to try to comfort her and have never had her do the task that caused the problem. The last straw came when Jess's little brother hit his mother and got upset when he was sent to his room because Jess has never gotten in trouble for hitting. Maggie and Dan decided to make a house rule that any aggressive behaviors from any of the children would lead to an immediate time-out. They sat the children down and made up a list of aggressive behaviors, which including hitting, throwing objects, and screaming at a person, that would no longer be allowed in the Jones household. They explained to the children that if they did these things, they would have to sit quietly in the bathroom for ten minutes. The ten-minute period wouldn't start until the child was quiet, and when time was up (which a parent would announce), the child would have to say what he or she would do differently next time.

The first time-out was used three days later when Jess hit Dan when she didn't want to eat her vegetables. Dan immediately took Jess to the bathroom and told her that she should sit quietly for ten minutes. Jess yelled and hit the door, and each time she came out, Dan or Maggie would take her straight back to the bathroom. It took forty minutes before Jess was quiet and Dan was able to start the ten minutes. At the end of the time, Dan went and opened the door and asked Jess what she would do differently next time. Jess replied, "Not get mad" and she then went back to the table and ate her cold vegetables.

The next time Jess was sent to time-out it only took her five minutes to sit quietly. Over several weeks, the number of times Jess was sent to time-out dropped from five in the first week to once in a two-week period. Maggie and Dan finally felt like they could work on Jess facing her fears without someone getting hurt.

REMOVAL OF PRIVILEGES

If further punishment is necessary beyond a time-out agreement, then removing a privilege is the next best thing. When a privilege is removed, it needs to have a meaningful and fairly immediate impact. For example, telling a child in October that there won't be any Christmas presents will not work nearly as well as telling the child that he or she cannot watch a favorite television program in half an hour. Privileges should never be removed for more than a few days as the impact will be lost, and it is likely that it will be too difficult for you to follow through and not give in. As with all our other strategies, communication is essential, and children need to know clearly why they lost the privilege and when they can get it back.

NATURAL CONSEQUENCES

Sometimes the things that anxious children do to express their anxieties have a natural consequence. For example, a child who decides to back out of going to a party should be responsible for phoning and saying that he or she cannot attend. If there are natural consequences to an undesirable anxious behavior, then allow your child to experience that consequence; do not protect him or her from it. In Jess's example above, having to eat her vegetables cold was a natural consequence of her behavior.

PARENT ACTIVITY: RESPONDING TO MY CHILD'S POSITIVE AND NEGATIVE BEHAVIORS

Having read all of this information on managing your child's anxiety, you need to start putting in place the ideas that you think are most appropriate for your child and family. There are two different approaches provided.

The first form is useful once you have identified the parenting "traps" that you have fallen into. Record each trap, what you intend to do differently when interacting with your child, and then your daily success in changing your interactions. Consider recording both your comfort in changing your reaction and how your child responded. Do not try to change many things at once; focus on one or two at a time.

The second is a monitoring form that you can use to follow your attempts to respond to your child's positive and negative behaviors. Over the next week, keep track of which of the helpful and unhelpful strategies you use. This will help you to become aware of where you need to change in your own interactions with your child.

Both of these tasks will help you to increase your awareness of how you can change your responses to your child's anxiety and, when making those changes, how his or her behavior shifts.

CHANGING MY APPROACH

What parenting trap am I currently falling into?	What will I do differently?

How successful was I?
Sunday:
Monday:
Tuesday:
Wednesday:
Thursday:
Friday:
Saturday:

RESPONDING TO POSITIVE AND NEGATIVE BEHAVIORS

What is it that my child did?	What action did I take (praise or punishment)?	What happened when I did this (what was my child's response)?

WHAT TO DO WHEN YOUR CHILD BECOMES FRIGHTENED

You may be wondering at this point, how do I stop my child from feeling anxious at those times when he or she suddenly becomes very scared and refuses to do something? The simple answer is, "You don't!" It is not possible to take away all of a child's anxiety. We all feel anxious at times, and we all need to learn how to deal with it. Even though it's really hard to see it in our own children, as parents, we sometimes have to accept that our children will feel anxious. When children get really scared for some reason, it is usually important to give them lots of contact, comfort, and security. Also, as we discussed earlier, it is very important for you to stay cool and calm so you don't add to the problem. Finally, we describe here a very structured way of helping your child to control his or her panic and begin to calm down.

A Problem-Solving Approach

Use of a problem-solving approach in handling children's anxiety has two advantages. First, it encourages a collaborative approach to solving the problem where both you and your child can influence the outcome. Second, it encourages children's independence in managing their own anxiety by giving them some of the responsibility. There are six steps to the problem-solving approach.

1. **Summarize what your child has said.** Check the accuracy of your understanding of the problem—that is, make sure that you know what your child actually means. Don't try and argue; rather, communicate your empathy with your child in a sympathetic but calm way.

2. **Identify what can be changed.** Ask your child what he or she can change—the situation, his or her reaction, or both.

3. **Ask your child to brainstorm all the possible ways in which his or her anxiety might be reduced.** Make sure you don't just take over the task for children. Rather, help him or her to come up with his or her own suggestions of ways to reduce the anxiety and feel better. Naturally, you will need to do more of the task for younger children and leave more of it up to older children. Also praise children for the ideas that they've generated. Even if the ideas are not actually very useful, praise them for their effort. The fact that they're engaging with you in the process of trying to constructively reduce their anxiety is a very positive and important step. Encourage your child to think of his or her detective character and to use detective thinking as one option.

4. **Go through each idea or strategy that your child has come up with, one by one.** For each idea, ask the child, "What would happen if you did this?" If the child doesn't know, gently point possibilities out to him or her (for instance, you might say, "I wonder if _____ would happen if you did _____ to make yourself feel better. What do you think?"). Remember, your overriding goal is to encourage your child to find solutions that involve approaching the situation rather than avoiding it. Praise your child for trying to come up with outcomes for each strategy.

5. **Ask your child to choose the strategy that is most likely to get the best result.** Remind your child of the evidence from detective thinking. You may find it helpful to have your child score each strategy on a scale of 1 (not at all helpful) to 10 (very helpful) to help him or her choose the strongest strategy.

6. **Later, once your child has tried the strongest one of the strategies, evaluate its success.** Discuss it with your child and consider what was successful, what was difficult, and what your child learned that could be used next time.

JESS'S EXAMPLE

Jess's parents, Maggie and Dan, are going out to dinner to celebrate their wedding anniversary. Jess is extremely worried about the potential of an accident happening while they are out. She is crying and clinging to her parents, begging them not to go.

Step 1: *Maggie and Dan sit down with Jess to find out what the problem is.*

Maggie: Jess, we can see that you're very upset about the idea of us going out. Can you tell us exactly what it is that is worrying you?

Jess: I don't know. I just don't want you to go.

Dan: Okay, we know that you don't want us to go. But we need you to tell us why. What is it that you are afraid will happen if we go out?

Jess: You might be in an accident and be hurt.

Maggie summarizes and checks her understanding of what Jess has said.

Maggie: So, you don't want us to go out because you think that we might be in an accident and get hurt. Is that right Jess? Is that why you're so upset?

Jess: Yes.

Step 2: *Maggie and Dan present Jess with her choices.*

Dan: Okay, Jess, your mother and I are going out tonight. And it's really up to you how you deal with that. You can keep on doing what you're doing right now, and feel really bad. Or you can try to do something to cope with the bad feelings that you're having. Mom and I would really like to help you cope with the bad feelings. Are you willing to give that a try?

Jess: I want you to stay with me at home. If you stay, I won't have any bad feelings.

Maggie: Jess, you've heard your dad. We're not going to stay at home with you tonight. The decision you have to make is what you're going to do about how you're feeling right now. How about you work with us and we'll try and come up with a plan to make you feel better?

Jess: I guess. . . .

Dan: Good girl.

Step 3: *Maggie and Dan prompt Jess to generate some suggestions as to how she might cope with her anxiety (that is, what she might do to make herself feel better). Jess is praised for her effort.*

Maggie: Okay, Jess. We need to think of as many things as possible that you could do that might make you feel better. What do you think you could do?

Jess: What do you mean? I don't understand.

Dan: Well, for instance, you're worried about us going out because you're saying to yourself that if we go out, we might have an accident. Maybe instead, you could watch a video and take your mind off your worries. Do you see what I mean?

Jess: I could take your car keys and hide them. Then you wouldn't be able to go.

Maggie: Well, that's one idea. At this stage, we'll write down all the ideas and then we can decide on one later on.

Jess: I could go and watch my video to take my mind off things.

Dan: Great, Jess. What else could you do?

Jess: I could write down that thing about you and Mom being good drivers, so that I can remember it later.

Maggie: You mean your detective thinking—that's really excellent, Jess. You're trying really hard and coming up with some good ideas. Can you think of anything else?

Step 4: *Maggie and Dan prompt Jess to identify the likely consequences or outcomes of each of the coping strategies she has come up with.*

Dan: Right. Now Jess, we've got a few different ideas written down here about what you might do to make yourself feel better about us going out. Let's go through them one at a time and find out what would happen if you actually did each of these things. First of all, there was the idea that you hide the car keys. What do you think would happen if you did that?

Jess: You might stay home?

Dan: You know, Jess, I think that if you did that, it's probably more likely that we'd send you to your room and call a taxi to take us out to dinner.

Jess: Yeah, I guess.

Dan: How about your idea about watching a video? What would happen if you did that?

Jess: I'd have fun and I wouldn't be thinking about you and Mom.

Dan: How about your idea of writing down that your mom and I are good drivers? What do you think would happen if you did that?

Jess: It would remind me that you probably wouldn't have an accident, and I might feel better.

Maggie: Okay, that's the end of our list. Well done, Jess. You're doing a really excellent job of helping yourself get over your bad feelings.

Step 5: *Maggie and Dan prompt Jess to choose the best solution.*

Dan: Okay, now the last thing we need to do is to pick one of these ideas. Have a look at the list and the things that would probably happen if you chose each idea. Which one do you think would be the best for you?

Jess: Well, that's easy. It would be my idea of watching the video. Plus, I could also write down something about you and Mom being good drivers, to remind myself not to worry.

Maggie: I think that's an excellent choice. Your dad and I are very proud of you for being able to figure out how to cope with your worry in a helpful way.

Step 6: *Assuming that Jess handled her anxiety in a useful way and allowed Dan and Maggie to go out without further difficulty, they would praise her efforts the next morning and evaluate the usefulness of the strategies. They might also organize a special reward to acknowledge her bravery, such as playing a favorite game with them.*

Maggie: I'm so proud of the way that you handled yourself last night, Jess. Not only did you deal with your worries, but you did the things that we agreed to and got through the night without even calling us.

Jess: Yeah, Sally [the babysitter] and I made some popcorn to watch with the movie. The movie got a bit scary, and we both hid under the pillows!

Maggie: It sounds like you had a great time. What did you learn from what we did?

Jess: That if you find something good to do, eventually the worries don't bother you so much.

Maggie: What about the detective thinking?

Jess: That helped when I thought about you guys at bedtime. I started to get worried again but I just said to myself, "Dad's a good driver, and they're only ten minutes down the road."

Maggie: Very well done. You even came up with some evidence of your own. Is there anything that you would do differently next time?

Jess: Yeah, I'd get some chocolate to go with the movie!

That evening Dan went bike riding with Jess to reward her for her efforts the night before.

The completed problem-solving worksheet from this situation would look like this:

Step 1: What is the problem?	Mom and Dad are going out, and I don't want them to go	
Step 2: What can you change?	I can change my reaction; they are going out even if I don't want them to.	
Step 3: Brainstorm ideas for solving this problem.		Step 4: For each idea—what would happen if you did it?
Solution 1:	Take the car keys and hide them.	I'll get in trouble, and they will get a taxi.
Solution 2:	Watch a video to take my mind off it.	I'd have fun and wouldn't be thinking so much.
Solution 3:	Write down some evidence for my worries.	I wouldn't be thinking about accidents and I might feel better.
Solution 4:	I could have a big tantrum.	I'll get sent to time-out and end up more upset.
Step 5: Which idea is best? Which is second best?	I'll use 2 and 3: first do some detective thinking and then watch a video.	
Step 6: Evaluate how your idea worked—what would you do next time?	My worries stopped once I started to enjoy the video and as a reward I got to go bike riding with Dad. My solutions worked well.	

PARENT ACTIVITY: PROBLEM SOLVING

For the situation your child most commonly gets anxious in, jot down some ideas for each step of the procedure outlined in the reading. Try to preempt any problems that you might have at each step.

Step 1: What is the problem?	
Step 2: What can you change?	

Step 3: Brainstorm ideas for solving this problem.		Step 4: For each idea—what would happen if you did it?
Solution 1:		
Solution 2:		
Solution 3:		
Solution 4:		

Step 5: Which idea is best? Which is second best?	
Step 6: Evaluate how your idea worked—what would you do next time?	

ACTIVITIES TO DO WITH YOUR CHILD ...

CHILDREN'S ACTIVITY 15: REWARDS

Begin by getting your child to tell you what a reward is. Make sure that you remind your child that rewards are not only for success but also for effort. Next, brainstorm as many rewards as you can together and list them on paper. To help you come up with a long list, here are some suggestions:

- Going out for lunch
- Renting a video
- Buying a CD
- Pizza delivered
- Sleepover
- Extra-late bedtime Saturday night
- Magazine
- Special activity (for example, movie, minigolf)
- Planning and preparing a dinner party
- Going on a family picnic
- Visiting grandparents
- Hobby supplies
- Inviting friends over
- Mystery trip
- Going to a community activity
- New clothes
- Trip to a bookstore

- Pieces of a construction set
- School effort awards
- Bike ride with parent
- Tokens that can be saved for big rewards
- Having a TV in the bedroom for a night
- Using a camera to make a scrapbook
- Own garden
- Camping out
- Bubble bath
- Swimming
- Stickers
- Playing board game or cards with parents
- Kite flying
- "I'm proud of you" card through the mail
- Lunch order
- Poster for bedroom

Once you have a large list, have your child identify rewards that he or she would like to work toward. Ask you child for ideas of fun things to do with the family, things he or she would like to hear (such as praise from Dad), activities to do at home, and material goods to work toward. Let your child identify unrealistic and realistic rewards at this stage; you can negotiate which rewards are used when you work on creating stepladders. Remind your child that rewards can be for success or for big efforts.

CHILDREN'S ACTIVITY 16: REWARDING YOURSELF

Talk with children about how *they* can also give rewards by talking to themselves in a positive way or by doing something that makes them feel good. Use examples to help your child understand, such as saying, "Way to go; that was a great goal!" or by doing a favorite craft activity after spending time practicing a new skill like detective thinking. Ask your child to think of ways to self-reward for recent successes or big efforts. You may first need to practice with examples, such as, "What could you say to yourself if you helped a friend solve a difficult math problem?" or "What could you do to make yourself feel great after you learn how to dive into the swimming pool for the first time?"

Self-rewards are important as a way of helping your child become self-motivated. Once again, make sure that your child understands the point that it is his or her effort as well as the achievement that can be rewarded. We do not succeed all of the time but if we try our best, then we have a sense of accomplishment to take away with us.

CHILDREN'S ACTIVITY 17: LEARNING TO SOLVE A PROBLEM

This activity is about learning how to solve a problem using a structured worksheet. You will need to create a worksheet of your own based on the example from earlier in the chapter or use the one provided in the workbook at www .ceh.mq.edu.au/hyac.html. Explain to your child that problem solving can be used when he or she isn't sure of the best thing to do in a situation. Using Jess's example described earlier, show your child how it is possible to brainstorm solutions for a problem and then evaluate what would happen if you did each possible solution so that you can choose the best one to try. Have your child think of another solution that Jess might have considered, and work out what the likely consequences would be to that solution.

Explain the steps of problem solving, including the following:

1. Write down the problem.

2. Work out if you can change your reaction, the situation, or both.

3. Brainstorm solutions.

4. Work out if each idea would lead to a good or bad outcome.

5. Choose the idea that would work best (or a combination of ideas).

6. Put the plan in place and afterward evaluate how well the plan worked. If it didn't work, you go back and try some of the next-best possible solutions.

Using a blank worksheet, choose a problem that has recently been faced by your child or create a hypothetical problem (for example, getting invitations from two friends for the same day and having to resolve how to deal with this while not wanting to hurt either person) and have your child work through the problem-solving steps. To start with, choose a simple problem that is not too closely related to your child's current anxieties. Be sure not to become critical of your child's suggested solutions or past behaviors—never use the words, "Well, wouldn't that have been a better way to behave than bursting into tears yesterday!" Your only response to your child's ideas should be praise and encouragement for the effort.

Once your child has gotten the idea, you can try to use problem solving as a skill to help manage anxiety in difficult situations.

CHILDREN'S PRACTICE TASK 3: REWARDING YOURSELF

The focus of this practice task is on getting your child to monitor the good things that he or she does during the week and to record the self-rewards for doing these things. Use the table in the workbook or create your own chart where your child can record what he or she did, can rate how big or little that achievement was, and what self-reward he or she gave (all of which helps your child understand that big achievements and efforts get big rewards, while small achievements and efforts get small rewards). Your child could self-reward for activities like doing detective thinking, helping Mom with an extra chore, trying extra hard during a difficult school subject, or anything where he or she put in effort.

As situations arise, your child should also practice using detective thinking and problem solving (and you and your child should both reward such efforts).

CHAPTER HIGHLIGHTS

In this chapter, you learned ...

- The unhelpful strategies for parenting anxiety include:
    - Giving your child excessive reassurance
    - Being too involved or directive when your child attempts activities
    - Permitting your child to avoid age-appropriate activities
    - Becoming impatient with your child

- The helpful strategies for parenting anxiety include:
    - Rewarding brave, nonanxious behavior
    - Ignoring anxious behavior
    - Prompting your child to cope constructively
    - Modeling brave, nonanxious behavior

- There are ways to help distinguish between anxious behaviors and naughty behaviors, and useful ways for responding to naughty behaviors.

In this chapter, you and your child learned ...

- Providing clear and consistent rewards for your child can help to support and increase brave behaviors.

- Effort is as important as achievement when facing fears.

- When your child tries hard at something, he or she can self-reward with self-talk or special activities.

- You and your child can use collaborative, structured problem solving as a way of dealing with difficult situations.

Your child will need to do the following:

- Keep a record of all the good things he or she did and the ways in which he or she self-rewarded. Make sure you ask your child about this worksheet from time to time; make extra sure that you go through it with your child at next week's anxiety management session and that you praise his or her efforts.

- Continue to practice detective thinking and filling out the Detective Thinking worksheets at least once per day. Your child should do this with respect to any situation that makes him or her even a little anxious and should also be encouraged to use the detective thinking technique as much as possible throughout the day whenever he or she notices anxiety increasing.

- Take the opportunity to use collaborative problem solving to find a solution to any problems that arise during the week.

CHAPTER 5

Facing Fear to Fight Fear

UNDERSTANDING STEPLADDERS

Detective thinking will have taught your child different ways to think about things that worry him or her. This is an important first step in managing anxiety. However, learning new ways of thinking about a situation is not enough by itself to overcome worries and fears. Thinking realistically is not much use if the old ways of behaving don't change as well. It is now time for your child to try out his or her new ability to deal with fears and worries in real situations.

Stepladders are a way to help children overcome their fears by facing up to the very things they are scared of. It's mostly a commonsense procedure, and you will probably find that you have tried something like it before. The difference here is that we will put it into an overall anxiety management plan, and we will show you how to be more structured in the way you approach this strategy. Stepladders are carried out in a step-by-step fashion so that it isn't overwhelming for your child. In this way, your child will experience difficult situations gradually and learn to cope with them. Being encouraged to try things that are frightening, and learning to cope, will give your child confidence and help to break the pattern of automatically responding with fear and worry.

Avoiding Fears Doesn't Help

There is an old story of two men walking along the street, one man stopping every few steps to bang his head on the sidewalk. Finally his friend can stand it no more and says, "Will you stop hitting your head on the sidewalk?" The first man answers, "I can't; it keeps the crocodiles away." His friend says, "But there are no crocodiles here!" The first man smiles and says, "See?"

Anxious children will avoid many apparent dangers that just aren't very likely to happen when we look at them rationally. However, by continuing to avoid, the child never learns that his or her behavior has nothing to do with the outcome. For example, just think of a child who is frightened of being killed while sleeping and so wants to sleep with his or her mother and father every night. We all know that the chance that the child will be killed while sleeping is almost zero. But by sleeping with his or her parents every night, the child never actually learns this. Logically convincing the child that he or she won't be killed is the goal, and using detective thinking is the first step. But this is not enough. The child must actually face the fear to *really be convinced* that being killed at night just won't happen.

Avoiding things actually strengthens the anxious beliefs, making it increasingly difficult for children to do things. Most anxious children have developed ways to avoid situations where they might become anxious. Sometimes these avoidance strategies can be very subtle and so habitual that even parents can be unaware of them. Stepladders give your child opportunities to practice different ways of behaving and learn that he or she really is able to cope with the fear.

The same ideas apply to all types of fears, whether they are fears of being separated from parents, fears of specific objects (e.g., heights, spiders), or excessive worrying about social situations or performance in a school test. The particular things being faced up to might differ, but the basic principles remain the same.

Let's look at an example of how you might try to overcome a fear of your own using stepladders. Suppose you were afraid of public speaking and you wanted to become more comfortable with this so that you could take a promotion at work that involved giving talks to large groups of people. Naturally, you would begin by doing your realistic thinking—what is it that you are worried about, what is the evidence that this would happen, and so on. But this technique alone would not be enough. You would also need to face your fears. To begin with, you might decide to present a short speech to your family. This would perhaps be a little frightening because it might seem silly, but it shouldn't be too hard. Once you have done this step (perhaps more than once), you might decide that you are now ready to present a short talk to a group of friends. After this, you might practice doing readings and introducing speakers at your local club. The whole time you are doing these steps, you are practicing your realistic thinking. After a few weeks of practicing these easier steps, you should find your confidence starting to build. Your next step might then involve presenting a few practice talks to your work colleagues. At the same time, you might join a public speaking club and practice giving weekly talks to the club members. Finally, you grab that promotion and begin to give talks as part of your new job. Even here, you could break things down by organizing your schedule so that your first talks are to smaller and less important groups and your later talks are the really tough ones. By gradually and systematically building up to your final goal in this way, you will become used to public speaking and will learn that you can cope and that the terrible things you may have imagined before are just not very likely. Over a period of weeks (or even months) you will find yourself becoming less and less worried about presenting in public.

Exactly the same principles apply when you begin to do stepladders with your child. For example, let's think of a child who is afraid of going to sleep in the dark and wants the lights on in his or her room every night. To do stepladders, you might first get the child to go to sleep with a fairly bright light on in the hall. If this is not too big a step, the child will most likely agree. After several nights, you might get the child to go to sleep with a light on in the room across the hall. Then, after a few nights, the child might agree to try a small, fairly dull lamp in the hall outside. Eventually, the child could try going to sleep with the only light being a very faint one in a distant room. Finally, the child will go to sleep without the light on at all.

At each step, the child will undoubtedly be a little anxious. But by gradually reducing the light in this way and having small enough steps, the child can reach the final goal without ever having to face extreme fear.

How Do Stepladders Work?

Stepladders are a step-by-step way to beat fears. With your help, your child will work out a step-by-step plan to beat each fear. Your child will attempt each step in turn, beginning with the least difficult and working up to situations that are the most worrying.

Every step of a stepladder is more proof that your child can beat the fear. He or she will feel proud of his or her success as he or she conquers each step but will need your encouragement to keep going. A system of rewards can be negotiated between you and your child to provide extra incentives to keep trying. To remind yourself about the ways to use rewards, see the section "Rewarding Brave, Nonanxious Behavior" in chapter 4.

Children learn from stepladders that even if they feel worried, they can cope. During a stepladder, children will have to experience some situations that make them feel worried. This is important because it helps children learn that although they may have started off feeling uncomfortable and worried, the bad things they feared did not actually happen. By doing this, your child learns that he or she can tolerate some feelings of worry and that these won't stop him or her from doing things. After all, none of us can go through life without ever feeling anxious.

Practice is the key to success. It is not enough to practice a step just once. Your child will have to repeat each step over and over until the situation no longer causes a lot of anxiety.

How You Can Help

Anxious children lack confidence in their ability to manage certain situations. They may believe that they are less capable or weaker than other children. Children's past experiences may make them reluctant to try something new or something they may have "failed" at before. You are going to have to encourage your child to try to do things that will not be easy. You will need to be sympathetic and understanding, but at the same time, you will have to be tough. This won't be easy. But remind yourself that it is for your child's good in the long run. At times, it may help to read over chapter 4 on parenting an anxious child.

BELIEVE THAT YOUR CHILD CAN DO IT

You may be worried about your child's capacity to tolerate anxiety and discomfort. For example, you might feel that he or she is more sensitive than other children. Children can pick up subtle messages from parents about how capable they are or how difficult a certain task may be. For this reason, it is important that you don't let your worries show. Be positive about what your child is trying to. change.

ARE YOU WORRIED TOO?

As a parent, it can be very difficult to know when to be sympathetic and help children out and when to ask them to try a little harder. This can be extra difficult for parents who may have similar fears. You know that it is good for them to do it but you may also feel empathy with the worries your child has and feel inclined to protect him or her. If you feel like this, it's understandable. But you will have to try and separate your own concerns from those of your child. It may help to do your own realistic thinking about the problem. As we discussed in the previous chapter, it is also often a good idea to model for your child how you are coping. You can do this by setting your own stepladders so that you and your child can work on them together.

When your child begins to do stepladders, you may well find this quite difficult to face. There will be times when you will be sending your child out to face some pretty difficult situations and possibly to become quite frightened. At these times, many parents feel guilty and torn. If this is a risk for you, you need to try and put some safeguards into place to help you through this part of the program. First, remind yourself that encouraging children to face their fears is good for them and is the only way they will overcome their fears. Next, brainstorm some ways in which you might help yourself feel better at those times when you feel bad. For example, you might write out a Detective Thinking Worksheet for your own beliefs and worries at these times and read over it to remind yourself of the more realistic beliefs. Or you might make sure you have plenty of work to get into to distract yourself from your guilty thoughts. Alternatively, you might be able to ask for support from your partner or a good friend. These people might be able to remind you that you are doing the right thing and that your child will not "break" or "hate you" for what he or she is going through.

In short, these feelings are completely understandable but need to be overcome for the good of your child.

BE CLEAR ABOUT WHAT YOU EXPECT

It's important to be clear in your mind about what are reasonable expectations for children of your child's age and for your child particularly. Your child will be best helped if you are clear on what you expect him or her to be able to do and how much you will help. For example, it would be unrealistic to expect a six-year-old child who is afraid of being away from Mom to stay home alone in the evening. But it would be quite reasonable for a fifteen-year-old to do this. In a similar way, there might be different expectations for children in different areas. For example, expecting your child to walk home alone from the bus stop might be quite reasonable in certain neighborhoods but not in others. Talk to other parents or your child's teacher if you are unsure about what you should reasonably expect from your child. In addition, if you have a partner or someone else who also cares for your child, make sure you sort out these expectations together so that you are in agreement about what your child should do. It is very difficult for children to learn not to fear certain things if they are getting different messages from their caregivers.

STEPS TO TEACH CHILDREN STEPLADDERS

Developing stepladders with your child is usually fairly straightforward. But it can be tricky at times, and, as with any skill, there are some systematic steps you can follow that can make it more likely to work.

Step 1: Explaining Stepladders to Children

The first step in facing fears with your child is to explain clearly and simply the purpose of the exercise. It's important that your child is a willing and active participant in the process, or you will be fighting an uphill battle. Naturally, the way in which you explain stepladders will vary a little depending on your child's age.

A useful way of explaining stepladders to children is to tell them a story of a child who is scared of something very straightforward (like a fear of dogs or a fear of heights) and ask them to suggest some ideas on how they could help that child overcome those fears.

A good example is to describe a child who is frightened of swimming in deep water. Ask your child how he or she might suggest to that child how to go about getting used to going into the water. Most children are pretty good at coming up with a commonsense plan. Hopefully, your child will be able to come up with a plan where the other child would begin with a low-fear step (for example, going into water up to his or her knees). If your child does not come up with a sensible approach, you will need to prompt gently until he or she gets the idea. The next suggestion might be for the child to gradually begin to move deeper and deeper into the water. This should allow time for the child to relax and get used to each step. Hopefully, children will understand that the frightened child will need to experience a little bit of fear, but by moving through each step gradually and getting used to each step along the way, that child will eventually reach the final goal without too much discomfort. Activity 18 about Molly and her fear of heights will help you to structure this introduction.

Step 2: Making a Fears and Worries List

Once your child understands the idea of stepladders in principle, the next step is to apply these ideas to his or her own specific difficulties. To begin, you and your child will need to sit and brainstorm all the different things that he or she is afraid of. You will create a Fears and Worries List that is a record of a number of different situations and activities that your child finds frightening and usually avoids. For example, items such as big dogs, meeting new people, and spending time away from you, could all be included. For some children there may only be one fear while for others there will be many. No doubt, you will have many suggestions and you will need to make sure that your child covers as much as possible. But it's important that your child is involved in the exercise, so encourage him or her to come up with the ideas first, if possible. Try to make this a fun game, seeing how many things you can list. Children may need to be reminded of specific situations where they may have been anxious rather than presented with a general concept such as fear of separation. It's also important that this is not seen as a list of failings but as a list of things they would like to be able to do.

At this stage the idea is to get your child involved and brainstorming. Therefore, don't worry if the suggestions are not realistic or even sensible. They can be fixed later. Also, don't worry if the list does not cover everything. The list can be added to later—it is a working reminder of what your child wants to change. As the items are generated, you will divide the list into things that are really hard, moderately hard, or not too hard. It is often a good idea for your child to give a worry rating for each item, although this is not essential at this stage. The most important point of this exercise is for you and your child to get lots of examples of the types of things that they don't do because of anxiety. Giving worry ratings to each item might simply help you to make sure that fears are roughly sorted.

You might find that your child isn't able to come up with fears or may even suddenly claim now to have no problems at all. It is not uncommon for anxious children to deny any difficulties. We call this "faking good" and it usually happens because your child wants to appear "perfect" both to you and to him- or herself. If you believe that your child is avoiding acknowledging his or her fears, don't nag. Begin by suggesting one or two recent situations that were difficult. Focus on the lower-level fears and remind your child that you will tackle those first and then come back to the list. Some children may avoid some areas of difficulty, such as social fears, but focus on others. Acknowledge that your child is working on one area and plan to try the other, more difficult problems later. As your child succeeds on easier problems, he or she will gain the confidence to try to beat some other worries. If your child still denies having any difficulties, challenge him or her to try certain things anyway. For example, you might say something like, "I think you are a little afraid of X, so why don't we put this down, and if you are not, then you can prove to me that I am wrong."

LASHI'S EXAMPLE

Lashi had many worries—and they seemed to be getting worse, upsetting everyone in the family. Lashi and her mother made a list of the main things she worried about. Her mom chose a quiet time when she and Lashi could talk about the worries. At first Lashi thought everything worried her equally, but when talking with her mother she was able to sort the worries into groups. Writing it down can make the fears seem more manageable.

FEARS AND WORRIES LIST

These things are really hard to do.	Staying with a sitter all night (9)
	Having an injection (10)
	Mom being late home or late picking me up (9)
	Worrying about burglars (10)
	Sleeping in my own room (8)
These things are hard to do.	Going to school (6)
	Going to the doctor with Mom (5)
	Hearing strange noises at night (7)
	Being in the dark (6)
	Staying over at Dad's place (5)
These things make me a little worried.	Being in another room at home (2)
	Going to a friend's house after school (4)
	Visiting Grandpa and Grandma with Mom (1)
	Visiting Dad's place for the afternoon (2)

Using this list of fears and worries, Lashi and her parents could choose which worries to start with to make step-by-step plans to fight her fears. The fears seemed to fall into three main groups—(a) being away from Mom, (b) being in the dark, and (c) going to the doctor, particularly getting an injection.

PARENT ACTIVITY: EXPLORING YOUR CHILD'S FEARS AND WORRIES LIST

As part of your anxiety management session this week, your child will be creating a Fears and Worries List. It can be helpful for you to think through what might appear on that list before the session.

These things are really hard to do.	
These things are hard to do.	
These things make me a little worried.	

How might these fears be grouped together, that is, how do the situations relate together or what are the common underlying fears?

_____

_____

_____

Step 3: Working Out a Step-by-Step Plan

Once you have listed as many fears as possible, the next step is to organize the fears into a practical plan. The aim is to have one or more stepladders—that is, lists of fears that are practical and organized so that they contain a number of steps going from the easiest to the hardest.

You will find that some of the fears that you have recorded on the Fears and Worries List are already small practical steps in and of themselves. For example, the item from Lashi's list, "Visiting Grandpa and Grandma with Mom" is rated as a low-level worry and is practical and doable. On the other hand, some of the items on your list will be much broader and larger. For example, from Lashi's list, the item, "Being in the dark" is quite vague and broad because Lashi's level of fear might be very different depending, for example, on whether she was inside or outside, which room she was in, what time it was, how dark it was, and so on. The items that are practical and doable, can be left as is. However, the items that are broad and a little vague need to be rewritten so that they are much more specific. This might involve breaking them down into several smaller steps. For example, the item, "Being in the dark" could be broken down into several different items such as "Being in my room with the light down low," "Being in my room with the light off in the early evening," "Being in my room later at night with the light off," "Being in the far room with the light off," "Standing outside the back door with the light off," and "Standing at the end of the garden with the light off."

When you have a detailed list consisting of specific, practical tasks, your child can place them in order of difficulty from easiest all the way up to the hardest. Once they are organized, you and your child will have your first stepladder.

If your child has lots of different fears, you may find it easier to create several stepladders. Each stepladder would contain items that logically go together and are relating to the same overall fear. For example, you might have one stepladder for being away from parents, another for mixing with people, and a third for sleeping in the dark.

In creating stepladders, you'll need to make sure that you and your child have come up with steps that are not too far apart. The idea is that eventually your child will begin with the first step on the ladder and practice that item until he or she is relatively comfortable with it. Then, your child will need to move on to the next item up the stepladder, and so on. If the steps are too far apart—if the next step is too much of a jump for your child—he or she will not be able to do it and could lose confidence.

The best way to create smaller steps to reach a goal is to think about several different ways that a child can face a situation. For example, a situation such as "asking directions from a stranger on the street" can include many different features that will result in quite different levels of anxiety. Directions could be asked from a male or a female, from an older person or a younger person, or from a person alone, a couple of people, or a group of people. Each of these variations would most likely produce different levels of anxiety for a shy child, and each child will be different. By brainstorming about these variations, you can produce a large number of steps that your child can then place into order of difficulty and put onto a stepladder.

Another important consideration in creating a stepladder is to choose items that are doable. After all, your child is eventually going to be asked to do each item on the list. Look over the list and remove any steps that are offtrack or perhaps not even possible. For example, if dealing with a fear of heights, climbing to the top of Mount Everest might really help, but it's not very likely to happen.

On the stepladders in the children's activities there are ten steps, but you can have more or less than that. There is no set number of steps to be included, but there should be enough steps to provide plenty of opportunities for practice. It is more effective to have a greater number of smaller steps to reinforce the learning than only a few large ones. Large steps and big jumps in the level of difficulty between items must be avoided. Each step should be very clear, with details of time to be spent, the place, and what is to be achieved. Use everyday activities to give your child opportunities to really do lots of practice. Tasks that are too elaborate or difficult to organize, demanding special efforts from parents, will rarely be done despite good intentions.

LASHI'S EXAMPLE

Lashi and her mom came up with a number of different areas that she was frightened of including sleeping over at various people's houses (including her father's), sleeping by herself at night in the dark, staying home with a sitter while her mother goes out, and going to school. To help organize all of her fears more easily, Lashi and her mother decided to create separate stepladders for each of these different areas. We show, below, part of Lashi's stepladder for learning to stay home while her mom goes out.

Lashi's goal: To be able to stay at home with a sitter without worrying about Mom being out

1. Stay home with Dad while Mom goes out for ten minutes.

2. Stay home with Grandma while Mom goes out for thirty minutes.

3. Stay home with Dad while Mom goes out for the afternoon.

4. Stay home with Grandma while Mom goes out for most of the day.

5. Stay home with a sitter while Mom goes out for the afternoon.

6. Stay home with a sitter while Mom goes out for most of the day.

7. Stay home with Dad while Mom goes out for the evening (a few hours).

8. Stay home with Grandma while Mom goes out for the night (until late).

9. Stay home with a sitter while Mom goes out for a few hours in the evening.

10. Stay home with a sitter while Mom goes out for the night (until late).

GEORGE'S EXAMPLE

Part of George's shyness also extended to a perfectionistic streak. George was so worried about what others thought of him that he tried not to make any mistakes. As a result, he often worried extensively about whether he had said or done the wrong thing and he often redid his schoolwork many times in order to get it just right. Below is part of one stepladder that George made up to tackle this problem.

George's goal: Not to be bothered by making mistakes at school

1. Intentionally call Mark (a close friend) by the wrong name.

2. Don't brush hair before school.

3. Draw a wobbly line on a page and leave it there.

4. Don't check an essay for mistakes before handing it in.

5. Make a deliberate mistake in a science project.

6. Intentionally hand in an essay with several spelling mistakes.

7. Answer a question in class when not 100 percent sure of the answer.

8. Intentionally return library books three days late.

9. Deliberately give the wrong answer to a question in class.

10. Don't do the correct homework.

George is very shy, so one of his worst fears was speaking in front of other people. The following stepladder was designed to tackle this problem. George did not begin work on this stepladder until after he had done several steps on most of his other stepladders. This was both because public speaking was not a very important goal for George and also because it was a harder topic to tackle than several of his other goals.

George's goal: To present a talk to the class

1. Prepare a talk—not to be delivered.

2. Prepare a short talk and practice alone, taping it.

3. Give a short talk to parents.

4. Give the talk again to parents and deliberately leave something out.

5. Give the talk to grandparents and mispronounce a word.

6. Give the talk to aunts and deliberately drop notes.

7. Give the talk to friends and family.

8. Give a longer talk to friends and family.

9. Ask a question of the teacher in class.

10. Give a two-minute report to the whole class.

11. Give a longer talk to the class.

12. Make an announcement to the whole school.

TALIA'S EXAMPLE

Talia's fear of water had meant that she missed out on a lot of fun activities like pool parties and holiday activities.

Talia's goal: To swim at the beach with friends

1. Go to the local pool and swim across the pool at the point where I can just stand up.

2. Go to the local pool and swim at the deep end with Dad next to me.

3. Go to the local pool and swim in the deep end alone.

4. Go to the beach and swim in the sheltered lagoon.

5. Go to the beach on a calm day and swim with Dad.

6. Go to the beach on a calm day and swim on my own up to shoulder height.

7. Go to the beach on a rougher day and swim with Dad.

8. Go to the beach on a rough day and swim to shoulder height.

9. Go to the beach and swim out and back on a boogie board on a calm day.

10. Go to the beach and swim out and back on a boogie board on a rough day.

JESS'S EXAMPLE

Although Jess has two close friends at school, she is scared of spending time with other children in case she loses her current friends. She worries about this constantly and has missed out on activities with other children because of her fear.

Jess's goal: To spend time with children other than Sally and Annie

1. Call Jill and ask her about some homework details.

2. Ask Madeline a question on the playground before school.

3. Ask Jill and Madeline to join Sally and Annie in a game of basketball.

4. Talk to Sally and Jill about going away together during the holidays.

5. During lunch on Wednesday, invite Madeline over for dinner on Friday.

6. Sit with Jill while eating lunch and then ask her to join Sally and Annie.

7. Walk around to Madeline's house after school to see if she is home.

8. Arrange to meet Jill and Sally at the mall to have lunch.

9. Invite Madeline, Jill, Sally, and Annie to go to the movies.

10. Go to a party when Sally and Annie won't be there.

11. Accept an invitation to visit someone else's house.

12. Invite Madeline and Jill for a sleepover.

There are several other types of stepladders that will be discussed in the next chapter. These are slightly trickier to create, but they help with fears that involve doing things to reduce worry, like when a child wears only certain clothes or washes his or her hands a lot. If these types of fears are the only ones that your child has, then you might want to read the next chapter now. However, it is preferable if the first stepladder you attempt to create is for a concrete fear where your child is directly avoiding an activity because the stepladders in this chapter are easier to design and are easier for your child to understand.

PARENT ACTIVITY: CREATING YOUR CHILD'S STEPLADDERS

Although you will be creating stepladders with your child's help, it is useful to think through the possible stepladders and steps in advance. Based on the Fears and Worries List, how many stepladders do you think your child will need? Think about some ideas *before* you work with your child to create his or her stepladders. For each of the possible stepladders, you should list your ideas for possible steps—but remember that your child should ultimately have a big say in which of these steps are entered on the final stepladder and the order in which they'll go.

WAYS OF MANIPULATING STEPS

- Group different tasks involving the same fear (for example, talking to relatives at the dinner table versus giving a presentation to the class).

- Change the number, age, gender, or familiarity of the people present while doing a step (for example, spending time in the playground with the sixth grade children versus spending time in the playground with classmates from fourth grade).

- Change items by the location of the task (for example, asking for help at the corner store versus asking for help at the customer service desk of a shopping mall).

- Change the amount of time spent in the situation (for example, staying at after-school care for a half hour versus staying at after-school care for the afternoon).

- Change the amount of preparation before going to an event (for example, being told on the previous Wednesday what will be happening on the weekend versus being told on Saturday morning what is happening on the weekend).

Step 4: Motivation and Rewards

Asking children to do stepladders can be like asking someone to have a tooth removed without anesthetic. Stepladders will be hard work for your child, and some steps can be quite frightening. By developing good stepladders with small steps, you can reduce the fear. But it isn't possible to get rid of it entirely. Your child is going to have to face fear to overcome fear.

We all need encouragement to help us to do unpleasant or difficult things. As an adult, you can recognize the value of unpleasant things; for example, if you have to undergo a painful operation, you would do it because you realize that it will help you in the long run. But children are not as good at recognizing what is good for them. One of the biggest differences between adults and children is that children have very little understanding of the future and the concept of time. Telling children, "You have to go through this pain now because it will be good for you later" just doesn't make the same sense to them as it generally does to adults.

For this reason, one of the really important parts of stepladders is to give your child rewards when he or she successfully completes a step (and to use backup rewards to encourage ongoing effort when your child tries a step but is unsuccessful). Giving rewards after each practice increases your child's motivation because it balances the unpleasantness of facing fears with a positive experience.

Over the years, we have occasionally come across some parents who do not feel that they should reward their child for doing stepladders exercises. After all, other kids can do these things without problems, so why should your child be rewarded for doing something that other kids do so easily? The point is that all children are different. For whatever reason, your child doesn't find these things easy, even though other children might. To put it in context, imagine forcing yourself to sing a song on national television or climb into a pit full of snakes. The level of fear you might feel doing these things is no more than what you are going to ask your own child to face. It is necessary for your child to do these things so that he or she learns to overcome these fears. But it won't be easy. Offering rewards for your child's attempts is the only way you will motivate him or her to try these things, and it will also communicate to your child your pride at what he or she is doing. A reward is not a bribe. Bribes are things you give someone to make them do something that is of benefit to you. A reward is simply a motivator to encourage your child to do something that will ultimately benefit him or her. A reward is also a signal of your delight and approval in your child's behavior.

We covered all of the important facts about how to give rewards in chapter 4 about parenting an anxious child so we will not go through it again here, but we urge you to reread the section, "Rewarding Brave, Nonanxious Behavior" to remind yourself of the important points. Here are some of the main points to remember:

- Rewards do not have to be financial, but can include fun activities.

- Rewards do not have to be large, but need to be relevant to your child.

- The reward should be an appropriate size for the difficulty of the step.

- Rewards need to be given as soon as possible after your child has done what he or she agreed to do.

- You need to be consistent—give a reward if your child has earned it but don't give it if the step hasn't been attempted.

- Reward your child for doing the step whether or not he or she was scared.

Step 5: Doing Stepladders

Once you and your child have brainstormed a series of situations that your child is frightened of, organized these situations into one or more stepladders, and decided on a few rewards for the first few steps of the stepladders, your child will be ready to begin facing his or her fears.

To begin stepladders, your child should pick the first step of one or two stepladders. You and your child will set a date and time that he or she will try a first step. How much you leave this up to your child's control will depend on the age of your child, the type of step, and what point you are up to in the program. For an older child, you may simply decide that he or she needs to do the step "some time this week." For a younger child, you might need to set the precise day and time. It is also a good idea to be more specific about practice early on in the program, for example, actually set a specific date and time for it—then you can loosen up a little and leave more control to your child later on, as he or she builds confidence. However, the control and timing will depend mostly on the type of step. Some steps will need to be set at a particular time (e.g., if the step involves you going out and leaving your child with a sitter), whereas others can be done more flexibly (e.g., leaving it up to your child to decide when to call for information on the telephone). Of course, some tasks will need to be more opportunistic and can only be done when the task presents itself (e.g., answering the telephone when it rings). Don't forget to reward your child when he or she has done the practice.

To help your child to get the most out of the stepladder, your child will keep a record of the week's plans and all of his or her practices (see "Children's Practice Task 4: Fighting Fear by Facing Fear"). This helps to make sure the practice is done and to let you know when practice is slowing down. It will also provide a great record of achievements that your child can look back on when his or her motivation begins to drop. This record also encourages children to think about what strategies they will use to manage their anxiety. And it allows you to track success and difficulties to keep track of your child's progress.

THINGS TO REMEMBER

The process of conducting an effective stepladder program involves being realistic, responsive, and repetitive, and rewarding effort and success.

Choose *Realistic* Goals

■ Choose goals that can be achieved and are appropriate to your child's developmental level and capabilities. The shy child will probably never become Mr. or Ms. Personality of the class but can aim to be able to speak up in class, give a talk, call to ask a friend over, and speak to the school principal.

■ Your child does not have to be totally free of anxiety. A certain amount of anxiety is normal and realistic in certain situations and may even help children to perform better. This program focuses on reducing *excessive* anxiety. Your child needs to learn that he or she can tolerate a certain level of anxiety and to go ahead and "just do it."

Respond by Adjusting the Program If Difficulties Occur

■ You need to monitor your child's progress and adjust the steps in response to the progress being made. It may be necessary to slip in new items to bridge a gap between the steps if there is reluctance to move to the next one. Sometimes the step can be altered by adding different people or varying the place where the task is to be performed. Moving through the items too quickly may mean the steps are not difficult enough. It may also be a form of avoidance since some children will just "grin and bear" a situation without learning that the situation itself is not too bad. You should talk to your child after each step and find out his or her attitude toward the situation. Doing stepladders should eventually produce an attitude like, "That's not so bad" or "I can handle that" instead of, "If I just hang in there, I can get through this."

■ Where there are difficulties or things do not go well at the first attempt, this too is a valuable opportunity to encourage your child to persist, to learn that a "failure" is not a disaster, and to look at how he or she might do it differently next time. When a child tries and doesn't succeed, you should still provide some form of backup reward for the effort. Remind your child about the earlier lessons on self-rewards—your child needs to remember that not everything has to be perfect every time.

Repetition Is the Key to Long-Term Results

■ It is important to remember that the best results and most long-lasting benefits from the program will come from lots of practice and repeating steps over and over until your child feels confident. You will know when your child has practiced a step enough, because you will get the feeling that your child could suddenly do that step again any time without warning and not get thrown at all. Look for a feeling such as, "I'm bored doing this step."

■ Repeating the steps strengthens children's learning of new ways of doing things by giving them more success and a growing feeling of mastery over the fear. Your child has probably had many experiences of feeling like "a failure." Trying the steps several times proves to children that they can do it and is essential to overcoming these well-established expectations.

Reward Effort and Success

- Maintain the reward program consistently throughout the stepladders process.

- Encourage your child to self-reward both for achieving a step and for his or her efforts in trying hard. You should keep up the praise and the rewards. Anxious children need reinforcement of their efforts to encourage them to keep going in the face of frustration.

- Good intentions to reward children for progress can be easily overlooked after some progress. However, the reward program and parental praise should be continued right through all of the steps of each stepladder.

As your child progresses up the first stepladder, you will be able to start on another of his or her stepladders. Children can usually work on two or three different stepladders at the same time.

ACTIVITIES TO DO WITH YOUR CHILD ...

CHILDREN'S ACTIVITY 18: FIGHTING FEAR
BY FACING FEAR

Remind your child that anxiety often changes what we choose to do or makes it much harder to give things a try. Then tell your child that fears can be stubborn and that they don't go away until you stand up to them. Tell the story of Molly, whose best friend is moving and is having a party in a restaurant at the top of Super Tower, the tallest building in the city. The problem is that Molly is scared of heights. Ask your child to come up with ideas of what Molly could do to make it possible to go to her friend's party (encouraging your child to come up with the idea of breaking the fear down by slowly having Molly go to higher and higher places). Repeat the activity of solving someone else's problem until your child seems to have a good grasp of the basic idea of breaking fears down and facing small amounts of fear at a time. You can use the following problems:

- Jeff won't play in the park or the yard because there might be a spider there.

- Adriana is afraid of the dark and still sleeps with the light on.

Explain to your child that with your help, he or she will be starting to face fears. Some children will be concerned about what they will be expected to try and how difficult it may be. When talking with your child, emphasize these things:

- You can create your own stepladders. All steps are negotiated, starting off with things you can almost do already, so it won't be too difficult. The harder steps will only happen once your confidence starts to improve, and then those steps won't seem so hard.

- Each step will be done a few times until you feel confident doing it.

- When doing steps, your anxiety will drop if you stay there long enough and also the more times that you do the step.

- You will be earning rewards as you move up your stepladders.

CHILDREN'S ACTIVITY 19: MAKING A FEARS AND WORRIES LIST

Similar to what you did earlier, help your child to create his or her own Fears and Worries List. It may be helpful to read through Lashi's example, found earlier in the chapter, before beginning so that your child understands that some fears listed will be ranked as only a little scary and others will be ranked as very hard to do.

CHILDREN'S ACTIVITY 20: MAKING YOUR STEPLADDERS

Continuing with Lashi's example, show your child how Lashi's fear of being away from her mom was turned into a stepladder. Emphasize that Lashi helped to plan these steps, that there were rewards for doing each step, that each step was repeated until Lashi wasn't really worried anymore by that situation, and that it was not until then that Lashi would move on to the next step.

Help your child to create a first stepladder by following these steps:

1. Set a goal that is practical.

2. List all the possible steps you can think of to break the worry down.

3. Give each step a worry rating (although this is not absolutely necessary).

4. Choose enough steps from your list so that almost all of the possible worry ratings have a step next to them.

5. Write your steps in order from easiest to hardest to create a stepladder.

6. Discuss what reward will go with each step (small rewards go with the little steps, and bigger rewards go with the harder steps).

When you complete the stepladder, praise your child for taking the first steps toward facing his or her fears.

CHILDREN'S PRACTICE TASK 4: FIGHTING FEAR BY FACING FEAR

Using the first stepladder (and any future stepladders that you create), your child now needs to commit to starting the first step. Talk about when, where, and how the first step on the stepladder will be attempted. Tentative plans for facing the second and future steps can also be made, but these depend on the success of the first step. Your child's fear will need to come down at least a bit on each step before he or she moves on to the next step. Make these initial plans with your child and then follow through during the week.

A planning and record table (with column headings, "What step will I do?" "When will I do it?" "What coping strategies will I use?" "Worry ratings before and after," "What I learned," and "What reward did I get?") can be very useful for keeping track of stepladder progress. You can easily draw a table like this yourself or you can use the form provided in the free workbook available from www. ceh.mq.edu.au/hyac.html. The strategies column is designed to remind your child to use other anxiety management skills, such as detective thinking, during the stepladder practices. Once you have the plans written down, you will need to follow through with attempts at the steps at the planned time. Ideally your child will be attempting a step or two every day (although remember that your child may need to do the same step four or more days in a row, perhaps, before he or she is ready for the next step).

In addition to having your child plan and record attempts at steps, it is also useful for parents to record the successes, challenges, and difficulties you experienced. To help with this task, a table is provided for you to use in the next parent activity. You can use these notes to work out any patterns to the difficulties your child is having. These patterns may help point to a solution. You can also use them to remind you of successes that your child is having over time.

PARENT ACTIVITY: MONITORING PROGRESS

It is important to monitor both your progress and your child's progress in implementing the agreed-upon steps. Use this table to record successes, challenges, and difficulties.

STEPLADDERS IN PRACTICE

What step was being attempted?	What problems were encountered?	What successes were achieved?

CHAPTER HIGHLIGHTS

In this chapter, you and your child learned …

- To fight fear you have to face fear.

- The best way to face fear is to break the fear down into small steps, with each step being a little harder to do than the last.

- To create a stepladder you need to do the following:

    - Set a practical goal.

    - List all the possible ways you could break the worry down into small steps.

    - Give each step a worry rating (this can often be useful, but is not absolutely necessary).

    - Choose steps that are practical and that cover low to high worry ratings.

    - Write the steps in order from easiest to hardest.

    - Set a reward for each step.

- Steps can be broken down by varying the type of task attempted, the people (or type of person) present, the location of the step, the amount of time in the situation, or the amount of preparation allowed before completing the step.

- It is important to plan when you will do steps and to keep track of successes and any problems faced.

Your child will need to do the following:

- Complete the children's activities with the help of a parent or other adult.

- Attempt the first step or the first few steps on his or her stepladder(s).

- Use detective thinking as a strategy to reduce anxiety when attempting a step.

CHAPTER 6

Simplifying Realistic Thinking and Creative Stepladders

At this stage of the program, your child should be working on challenging him- or herself by facing fears, gradually moving up a stepladder, and combining this with detective thinking. In this chapter we will give your child a way to make the detective thinking quicker and easier. We also introduce some stepladder approaches that address the unnecessary things children do to try to control their fear.

IN-YOUR-MIND DETECTIVE THINKING

As your child gets better at detective thinking, it is helpful to simplify the process so there's no need to complete an entire Detective Thinking Worksheet every time he or she gets worried. With new worries, particularly ones that are very distressing, the full process (in other words, using the complete original form) is important. However, you will also find that a lot of your child's worries are the same old ones going around again and again. In these cases, once your child has used the detective thinking successfully a number of times, he or she will be able to switch to using simple prompts to be reminded of the evidence.

Although there are many types of evidence you can look at when you do detective thinking (such as past experience, alternative

7upossibilities, etc.), we have found that many people will have one or two particular types of evidence that really work best for them. For example, your child may discover that asking, "What happened last time?" is the best way to change most of the worried thoughts into calm ones. Or it may be that thinking about past experience doesn't usually work too well for your child but that trying to find another explanation usually does work well. Discovering which thoughts and questions are most useful for your own child is a good way to make detective thinking work more quickly. Once your child has found one or two good questions and one or two good thoughts, he or she should record them on "cue cards" that can be used as a reminder of how to think or what to ask when he or she starts to feel nervous. This will make it easier for your child to manage anxious feelings independently. For example, your child may find the question, "What would Janice think?" (where Janice is a particularly confident friend) useful to ask when about to talk in front of other people. If your child has this question written on a small card in a pencil case, he or she can use it as a reminder just before answering a question in class. On the other side of the card, your child might write a realistic thought such as, "Lots of kids get some answers wrong, and it doesn't matter." Your child then has two prompts that can help when he or she is feeling worried. Importantly, your child can use these prompts without help from you or other adults, and these prompts can become a shortcut to helping remind your child of his or her calm thought quickly and easily.

There are two important points to remember if you are going to use this technique. First, the technique does not work for everyone and will only work for those children who begin to discover patterns to their worried thoughts and find the same (or very similar) thoughts coming up again and again. Second, these shortcuts will only work after your child has done the full detective thinking several times so that he or she really believes the evidence and understands where it has come from.

Finally, if your child has not been doing the full detective think-ing but has only been trying to identify calm thoughts, this technique can work just as well. As mentioned above, you may have found that there are a few particularly important calm thoughts that your child gets the most benefit from. These can also be listed on a cue card to help remind your child of these important thoughts.

DEVELOPING CREATIVE STEPLADDERS

Stepladders are an essential tool for overcoming fears and combating worry. Some fears are very concrete and are easily broken down into a series of steps. For example, a fear of dogs can be manipulated by changing the size, distance from, and activity level of a variety of dogs. Similarly, fears of separating from a parent can be manipulated by changing concrete factors such as the length of time away, the time of day, or the person doing the caregiving. However, some fears are much harder to break down into steps because they are not as concrete, and so working out how to manipulate steps can sometimes be quite difficult. In this section we will look at ways of addressing some of the more complicated and less obvious sorts of fears.

What You Need to Know to Create Successful Stepladders

As a first stage in developing stepladders for these less obvious fears, there are two questions you can ask yourself to help to make the source of the fear more concrete.

WHAT IS YOUR CHILD REALLY AFRAID OF?

This may sound like a silly question but consider this. You have a friend who is afraid of flying. That's how she describes it—"a fear of flying." If you wanted to work on a stepladder for this person, you might start with her reading about planes, then going to the airport, then walking on a plane, then taxiing in a plane, and finally going on a flight. Now this might work, but if it didn't, you would need to consider that fears of flying can actually involve several very different fears. Some people who are scared of flying are actually afraid of the flight itself—that is, they are afraid that the plane will crash. But others are more afraid of having to sit in those cramped seats, and they really have a fear of small spaces. Others are actually afraid of the fact that the plane is flying so high, and they have a fear of heights. So if your friend was actually afraid of being up that high, reading about planes and being on the plane while it's on the ground would not be of any use. When it came to taking off for the first time, however, she would still be terrified because she wouldn't have done any gradual steps to address her real fear of heights. Obviously, to create an effective stepladder you need to know what it is that the person is *really* afraid of; otherwise you might do a lot of steps but not get anywhere.

With children, working out what they fear in a situation is important, but it can also be difficult if they can't tell you what the problem is. At times you will need to experiment with different steps that cover different things that they *could* be afraid of until you find the ones that *do* cause their worry ratings to rise. It will be a matter of trial and error. A related "trick" might be to ask your child a set of hypothetical questions. In other words, ask your child to close his or her eyes and really imagine being in a situation that you will describe and then have your child tell you how frightened he or she would be. Then you can change the situation in various ways to work out what sorts of things make a difference to the level of fear. For example, with the situation we described above with your friend's fear of flying, you could have asked her to imagine sitting near the window or sitting near the aisle. If she was afraid of crashing, this really wouldn't make much difference, but if she was afraid of small spaces, she would probably be far more anxious jammed in next to the window. Similarly, if she told you she was more frightened looking out of the window than looking at the seat in front of her, it might tell you that she was afraid of heights since looking out of the window would make her much more aware of how high the plane was.

When working out what questions to ask your child, make sure you think of the situation from a child's-eye view. What a child understands the situation to be will be very different from your understanding of it. For example, say you are about to take your child on his or her first trip to the snow. Your child has never seen snow but loves vacations so is excited. As you start driving up into the mountains, your child starts to get upset while looking out the window. Your child starts crying, and you have to turn back. To you, there is not much that is frightening about driving in this area; you've done it before. To your child, these are the new things that he or she is dealing with: high rocks on one side of the car and a big drop on the other; signs that warn of falling rocks; strange-looking clothes and equipment; the noise from the chains on the car's wheels; and snow—which doesn't always look like the pictures in the travel brochures. There are a lot of things here that a child could be frightened by, while from your adult point of view, these things are expected. Take a moment to look at the world from your child's point of view—it can help you to work out what your child still needs to face.

WHAT IS YOUR CHILD AVOIDING?

Once you know what it is that your child fears, you then need to take yourself one step further and establish what your child avoids because of the fear. This can be particularly difficult if what he or she mostly does is worry about things. A child who's a worrier may avoid going into an unknown situation by asking many questions so that situation won't be an unknown anymore. You might just think of that child as a worrywart, but to help you develop stepladders, you need to think in terms of avoidance and realize that your child is avoiding anything that he or she does not know or cannot plan for.

In a similar way, your child might be very perfectionistic and work really slowly or check his or her work many times. But you need to think about what your child is avoiding—most likely a possibility of making a mistake. Or consider that the child who always sticks to the rules and does the "right thing" might be avoiding getting into trouble. There are a lot of possibilities for each fear. The key is often to look at the motivation for different actions. If you are unsure of what avoidance is going on, ask yourself for each of your child's actions, "Why is my child doing this right now? What is my child trying to avoid?"

When you know what the fear is and what your child has been avoiding, then you will be able to begin to create stepladders. The techniques listed below can help you to create appropriate steps when the fears are harder to grasp.

Response Prevention

We all understand avoidance when it involves *not* doing something. For example, children who won't go to school because they are afraid of leaving their mothers are pretty easy to understand. But in some cases, avoidance might involve actually doing one behavior in order to avoid another. This is often much harder to understand and identify.

A good example might be the child who is afraid of burglars breaking in at night. This child might check and recheck all the locks on the doors and windows every night before going to bed. In this example, the child is *doing* something—going around the house and checking. But notice that this behavior is still a type of avoidance— the child is avoiding the possibility that a burglar might break in.

A child who is afraid of germs provides a more complex example. This child might avoid touching certain dirty objects. This is obvious avoidance—the child is *not* touching. But that child might also wash over and over again, just in case he or she had touched something dirty. In that case, the child is also *doing* something—washing. But not doing something (not touching dirty objects) and doing something (washing repeatedly) are both types of avoidance—they are both aimed at that child avoiding contact with germs.

When a fear causes your child to do something to avoid it, like checking that the doors and windows are locked, you need to gradually get your child to stop doing that behavior. When your child builds a stepladder, stopping that particular behavior should be included among the steps. This is called *response prevention*—in other words, *stopping your child from doing an action that gives him or her comfort.* This type of stepladder is very commonly needed for children who have obsessive-compulsive disorder. But it is also very useful for children with many other fears, such as those who are very perfectionistic or those who seek a lot of reassurance. When you are trying to create stepladders for these issues, you are trying to reduce the way something is done or the number of times it is done. Below are some examples.

Kurt is afraid of having germs on his hands. Because of this fear he spends a lot of time washing his hands many times during each day. When he washes his hands, he has to do it in a certain way. Kurt first washes his hands all over, then the bottoms of his arms, then his hands again. After this first wash, Kurt washes the taps to make sure that he won't get germs from the tap when he turns it off. Once the tap is washed, he washes his hands again, then turns the tap off and dries his hands on a clean towel that he pulls out of the cupboard (which he opens with his feet). The whole process takes between three and eight minutes, and at the moment, Kurt has to wash many times each day. In the following stepladder, each step builds on the last, so when he moves on to step 2 he continues to do step 1 at the same time.

Kurt's goal: To not wash my hands for a whole day

1. Use the hand towel that is on the hook to dry hands.

2. When washing, do not wash arms; stop at wrists.

3. After washing taps, only rinse hands again; do not use soap.

4. Do not wash taps, just hands.

5. Do not wash hands before eating a cookie.

6. Open and close every door in the house, and then eat a sandwich.

7. Play basketball, take shoes off, and then make and eat lunch with Mom.

8. Go to the toilet and then eat tacos and lick sauce off fingers.

9. Only wash hands when having daily shower.

10. Go for forty-eight hours without washing at all.

Children with obsessive problems need to do more in their stepladders than most of us would usually do in our daily lives. For example, for Kurt's fear of germs, one step might involve urinating a few drops on his hands and then not washing it off. Most of us would never want to do this, but it is not actually dangerous, and to learn this lesson, children with these obsessive types of fears will need to do this until it no longer scares them.

Here is another example of a stepladder for a child who has to check three times that all of the doors and windows are locked before going to bed:

Goal: To go to bed without checking locks

1. Check all locks but only check twice.

2. Check all locks but only check once.

3. Check the locks in a different order than usual.

4. Only check the door locks.

5. Have someone else check the locks, but I am allowed to ask about each door.

6. Have someone else check the locks, but I can't ask about them.

7. Go to bed and not check at all.

8. Go to bed after deliberately leaving the doors unlocked.

In both of these stepladders, two things are done: first, the order in which a routine is done is changed; second, the person is prevented from doing the routine as often as he or she is used to. This type of approach can also be used for reassurance seeking and perfectionism.

Here is an example for a stepladder that is aimed at reducing the number of questions a child asks about homework:

Goal: To complete homework within twenty minutes

1. Do homework with Mom, answering each question before asking her about it.

2. Do homework with Mom, completing five questions before asking her to check it.

3. Complete whole sheet, keeping questions to the end.

4. Complete whole sheet; Mom can check but only to correct spelling.

5. Complete sheet; only do one rough copy.

6. Complete homework directly on worksheet.

7. Complete homework in forty minutes and cannot check the answers.

8. Complete homework in twenty minutes without checking.

9. Only complete ten minutes of homework and hand it in.

10. Don't practice spelling words for the whole week.

There are many times when stepladders will include steps that prevent a response; typical examples of such steps might be not sleeping in a parent's bed, stopping a child from constantly organizing objects into a pattern, covering mirrors so a child cannot check how they look before going out, and not allowing a child to talk about worries at bedtime.

Exposure to Consequences

Many children who worry also overestimate how terrible the consequences of a feared event will be. This overestimated fear leads them to avoid taking the risk of having the catastrophe happen by avoiding the original task completely or by taking care to ensure a reduction of the risk. For example, a child may take special care to find out what friends will be wearing when they all go out to ensure that he or she won't look different. This type of fear is particularly common in children who generally worry a lot and also in children who have social fears. To conquer these fears, children need to be exposed to the potential risks so that they learn not only that it is unlikely that the feared event will happen but also that if it does, it really isn't that bad and life will go on.

As an example, a child who is overly conscientious about appearance because of fears of looking different will need to start taking the risk of looking different rather than sticking to the rules observed from peers.

Goal: Not to be bothered by how I look when I go out

1. Go to school with socks scrunched down, not rolled down.

2. Go to school with a bit of hair not in ponytail.

3. Go to stores without smoothing or brushing hair.

4. Go to school with shirt not tucked in.

5. Go to friend's house in clothes that I wore yesterday.

6. Go to stores, with friends, wearing last year's styles.

7. Go to school wearing regular clothes on sports day.

8. Go to picnic wearing jeans and old T-shirt.

9. Go to school event wearing jeans and old T-shirt.

10. Go to stores in a tracksuit with messy hair.

In this example the "problem" clothes were very individual to this girl and what she saw as appropriate. Consequently, much negotiation was needed as to what risks would be taken. During implementation of the stepladder, her parents developed awareness of small avoidances, like spraying perfume on clothes that had already been worn. New steps consequently had to be developed and then implemented to help her progress.

A second situation where exposure to consequences can be appropriate is for children who avoid making mistakes. These children might check their work repeatedly or do the work very slowly. Getting them to stop checking (response prevention) or to do their work faster is a great first step, but it is not enough. All this will teach them is that they are pretty careful kids and so, even if they don't check, they probably won't make a mistake. But to really manage their anxiety, they need to also learn that even if they do make a mistake, it is not the end of the world. Therefore, their stepladder has to include actual mistakes in it—in other words, they need to be exposed to the consequences of making mistakes. An example of a stepladder about learning to accept making mistakes was included in George's examples in chapter 5.

When using exposure to consequences, it is especially important to include detective thinking about the implications of what really could or did happen. This is important because otherwise the level of worry may not reduce across the different steps. Sometimes children might believe that something really terrible happened when in fact it wasn't so terrible at all—so using detective thinking after the step is important. It can also be important to prepare teachers if a child who never makes errors suddenly begins to. You want teachers to notice and give the appropriate consequence, but you do not want them to overreact or express their disappointment or anger. Dealing with that kind of reaction would be a much higher step on any stepladder.

Exposure at School

Many fears that children have are intensified when they are at school, particularly social fears. Consequently the stepladders for these fears need to be completed at school. There are a number of difficulties when completing these stepladders, including checking on step completion, providing immediate rewards, and dealing with the many unknown factors introduced by the other children.

CREATING STEPLADDERS FOR SCHOOL

Stepladders that are done at school need to be simple and doable by the child on his or her own. It is usually only possible to do a single step each day (although that step could be done more than once during the day). As a reminder, it is useful to write the step for the day on a piece of paper that is put into the child's lunchbox or into their homework diary so that the child is prompted as to the details of what should be done. Steps should specify what a child will do (e.g., ask for a ball), who he or she will do it with (e.g., ask the gym teacher), and when it should be done (e.g., at recess). School stepladders often require research as to what steps are possible. For example, say you are trying to reach the goal of not worrying about breaking school rules and the step is to walk outside the appropriate play area. You will need to know where "out-of-bounds" is and to specify this in the step. Otherwise there may be confusion as to whether your child achieved the step or not.

INVOLVING TEACHERS

When attempting school-based stepladders, it is useful to have teachers directly involved, and they are often more than willing to assist. This is particularly important if the steps involve in-class behavior like answering a question (the teacher will need to be ready to call on your child when he or she puts a hand up) or if it involves deliberately making mistakes or breaking a rule like forgetting to bring library books back. In this last case, you want your child to experience the normal consequences of forgetting (like a reminder note and not being able to borrow books that week), but you don't want your child to be yelled at in front of the whole class for this "first offense." When involving teachers, you will need to get their view of the difficulties being faced and you will need to make it as simple as possible for them to implement the steps so as not to disturb the normal running of the class. Teachers will also have ideas for steps that you may not have thought possible.

Teachers may also be able to help monitor step completion. For example, say a step for a socially anxious child is not tucking in a shirt for the whole day. You may inform the class teacher by way of a short note in the morning that this is today's step and ask that they write a note back on whether it was completed. That way the class teacher is aware, but your child still has to risk being scolded by other teachers for being messy. By having the teacher let you know about step completion, you can be confident that your child is progressing or know where you need to adjust steps.

Occasionally you may come across a teacher who is less than willing to be involved with implementing stepladders. That teacher may feel that there is no problem, that it is not the teacher's or school's responsibility to help, or worse, think that you, as a parent, are the problem. In this case it may be better not to involve that teacher and either rely on your child's integrity or find a more sympathetic teacher or perhaps the school counselor to support your efforts from within the school.

REWARDS AT SCHOOL

Remembering that rewards are more effective when delivered quickly, it may be useful to create rewards that can be given at school wherever possible. Special snack-time treats that can be handed out by the teacher for step completion, or tokens that can be exchanged for rewards when your child gets home are effective. It may also be possible for your child to work toward school rewards like certificates. The most important thing is that the rewards are consistently given.

OTHER CHILDREN

When completing steps at school, other children, or at least their reactions, might become involved. This can bring in an element of extra risk in completing the step. When preparing your child for a step that might involve things going badly, such as getting teased after answering a question incorrectly, it is worth talking about what could go wrong and what that means before the step is attempted. This can be incorporated into the detective thinking about the worst possible consequences. At times steps may involve social skills that your child is not yet particularly confident at using, like being able to handle teasing. If this is the case, then developing these skills before attempting the step that uses them will be important. Developing social skills and assertiveness are covered in chapter 8.

Overlearning

When you take a fear to its extreme and really challenge the consequences, it can help consolidate the learning that takes place when you complete a stepladder. By doing the worst possible feared event, or by doing what seems very much out of the ordinary, your child can gather very convincing evidence that even when the worst occurs, nothing much happens that will be important after some time passes. In the stepladders described in the section "Response Prevention" above, each last step is something that most people would not normally do—like not washing for two days. However, if your child does do any of these last steps, he or she certainly won't be concerned about the original thing that was feared. This is called *overlearning,* and other examples of it include having a child who fears doing something embarrassing wear his father's oversized clothes to a shopping center or having a child who fears making mistakes deliberately answer every question wrong in a test. This last one will require you to also let go of the need for your child to achieve his or her best all the time. The lesson to be learned by doing this final step is that even when you really do "mess up," the worst that happens is a bad grade on the test and a not-so-good end-of-term report on that subject—the world certainly doesn't end and the child won't get held back, both consequences a child might have feared before working on stepladders. Your child might also learn that mistakes can be overcome so it is worth persisting. Overlearning is not a necessity for learning to manage anxiety, but it can bring about significant change in your child's fear and worry levels. The sense of freedom a child can get when he or she manages to do something "really crazy" is definitely worth the effort.

Spontaneous Practice

As your child gains more confidence and becomes used to the idea of taking steps, you and your child will come across opportunities for what we call *spontaneous practice*. "Spontaneous practice" refers to opportunities to practice facing fears that were not actually part of your child's stepladder but have just come up in your child's daily life. For example, if your child is shy and has a fear of meeting new people, you may be sitting in a park one day and notice another child shooting a basketball by him- or herself. Although this specific situation may not be on your child's stepladder, you should encourage your child to grab the opportunity to join the other child as a way of facing the fear of meeting a new person. If your child is hesitant, don't forget to help with his or her detective thinking and come up with a good reward for doing the spontaneous practice. In some cases, these opportunities may even be a few steps higher than your child is currently at on his or her stepladder. If your child is willing to try, he or she should be encouraged and rewarded. However, if your child is really too worried, don't force the issue—it may simply be too soon.

Other Resources

Use resources in the community, family, and school system to provide a wide range of stepladder situations. Most people are willing to assist children who are learning new skills and readily understand the basic concepts involved once they are explained. Encourage grandparents and others not to be too helpful and to allow the child to experience some anxiety to overcome fears. Even store clerks, park attendants, or bus conductors can be relevant in certain situations.

PARENT ACTIVITY:
FACING A FEAR OF YOUR OWN

As we discussed in the section "Modeling Brave, Nonanxious Behavior" (chapter 4), a great way of modeling anxiety management to your child is to actively face your own fears. It is even better when you get your child to help you design your stepladder or to find evidence. Take a simple fear of your own and work with your child on facing this fear. Use the same steps and materials that you are familiar with. Allowing your child to help you face a fear helps to make worry and fear seem normal, it shows the benefit of managing fear, and it gives your child a great boost in confidence—being the "expert" by helping Mom or Dad to do something is a powerful experience. It is a good idea to pace each other—set your goals together earlier in the week and then go over your achievements at the end of the week. If you do this, you can both monitor your efforts and get special rewards (maybe one of your chosen rewards can be your child making you a cup of tea in the morning—the more you involve him or her the better).

ACTIVITIES TO DO WITH YOUR CHILD ...

CHILDREN'S ACTIVITY 21: IN-YOUR-MIND DETECTIVE THINKING

Assuming that your child has had several weeks of practicing detective thinking, work with your child to identify the most useful thoughts and questions that help him or her to think more realistically when anxious. Have your child write these on a small cue card to be carried in difficult situations. Your child may need to write out more than one card, for example one to carry in a pencil case at school and one to have beside the bed at night. Each card may also be specific to the situation that causes anxiety.

CHILDREN'S ACTIVITY 22: REVISING YOUR CHILD'S STEPLADDER

After completing *two weeks* of working on stepladders, children and parents will both have a better understanding of how the facing-fear process works. This is a good time to revise your child's stepladders. With your child, examine the first stepladder to see if the steps have these qualities:

- *They are practical.* Are the next steps tasks that can be done within the next few weeks? Do both you and your child know exactly what the tasks involve?

- *They have worry ratings that are not too far apart and not too close together.* Over time, worry ratings can change, so it is worth checking fear levels for upcoming steps. If the next task seems very easy to your child, just one attempt at the step may be enough before he or she moves on to the next one. If the next task seems very difficult, then new intermediate steps should be added.

- *They are related to each other.* To effectively work from the easy steps to the harder steps, the steps need to relate to one another; that is, they need to relate to the same type of fear.

If you identify problems, work with your child to change the steps to overcome the problems.

CHILDREN'S ACTIVITY 23: CREATING NEW STEPLADDERS

It is very likely that you will need two, three, or even many stepladders to work through your child's different fears. Create stepladders for the next few and most important fears that your child needs to face. Make sure that your child has the greatest say in which fears are most important. Granted, they may not be your highest priorities, but it is highly likely that what your child chooses will be the fears that are giving him or her the most trouble. There will be time as your child's confidence grows to get to other fears that cause you concern.

Use the same process as the one that you used to create your child's first stepladder (see "Steps to Teach Children Stepladders" in chapter 5):

■   Set a goal.

■   List all the possible steps and variations.

■   Rate these on the worry scale.

■   Choose a set of steps that covers the full range of the worry scale and write these in order onto a stepladder.

■   Assign rewards for each step.

■   Finally, make plans to start on the first steps of the new stepladder.

CHILDREN'S PRACTICE TASK 5: DOING STEPS

Children need to keep working on their stepladders. Write down plans for what step will be done, when, and the skills that will be used to help your child to cope. You should try to make these plans at the beginning of each week to ensure that progress continues to be made. Remember that decisions on the steps that will be faced should be led by your child. If progress seems too slow, then the step choices can be discussed, but children should still feel that they are in control of the process. If your child really seems to not want to do the step, then this reluctance may suggest that the step is too large and an intermediate step should be designed. While practicing steps, your child should use the new cue cards and, when needed, should continue to use detective thinking and problem solving to reduce feelings of anxiety.

CHAPTER HIGHLIGHTS

In this chapter, you learned …

- How to create stepladders that address particular actions your child might use to reduce fear of something (such as checking homework too often or washing hands constantly). These stepladders might include "response prevention"—that is, stopping your child from using actions that their fear encourages them to do

- How to create stepladders that expose your child to feared consequences, such as looking different or making mistakes, to help your child learn that he or she will "survive"

- What to consider when stepladders need to be completed at school, including how to involve teachers, give rewards, and anticipate the reactions of other children

- How to take advantage of spontaneous practice to help your child face his or her fear

In this chapter you and your child learned . . .

- To identify the calm thoughts and evidence-finding questions that are particularly useful for your child

- To review stepladders regularly for steps that are not practical, too big, too small, or that do not fit well together

- To continue to create stepladders for each of your child's fears

Your child will need to do the following:

- Complete the children's activities with the help of a parent or other adult.

- Practice more steps from the first stepladder and begin steps from any new stepladders.

- Start using cue cards to shortcut detective thinking and continue to use the full detective thinking process when facing a new or difficult worry.

CHAPTER 7

Troubleshooting Stepladders

Learning to manage anxiety can be challenging. Stepladders are the most important component of overcoming anxiety. However, there are many ways in which stepladders can go wrong. We don't mean that you can harm your child. Rather, there are some ways of doing stepladders that are really effective and other ways in which they may be less effective. We now discuss some of the problems you might come across when using stepladders and some ways of overcoming these problems.

GETTING STUCK

With the gains they are making, regular praise from others, and the chance to earn rewards, most children enjoy stepladders and make rapid progress. However, some children may find the going tough, and things may not go as smoothly as you would like. Children may get stuck on a step and refuse to try the next one, they may move through the steps very slowly, or they may want to give up on the stepladders altogether. If this is the case for your child, there are several things you can try.

First, summarize the progress that your child has made so far by repeating the last few steps that he or she has successfully done. Use this opportunity to really praise your child for his or her efforts and the gains that have been made. You may need to repeat this process several times to build up your child's confidence in his or her capacity to face fears.

Next, revise the detective thinking skills in relation to the new step. In particular, look carefully for any underlying worries your child may have. There may be unforeseen worries that your child has not admitted to that need to be dealt with before your child can move on.

Third, brainstorm ways in which the next step can be broken down into slightly smaller steps. This is especially important if your child has been moving along well and all of a sudden has become stuck. In this case, it is very possible that the next step is just too big a jump.

You also need to think about your own role in the process. You need to think about your own attitudes and feelings toward your child's progress. Anxious children can be very sensitive to their parent's concerns. If you are personally worried about the next step or are not totally convinced about the value of stepladders, you may accidentally be giving your child subtle messages that are interfering with his or her progress.

Additionally, ask yourself whether you have been holding up your end of the bargain. Have you been rewarding your child as promised? Have the rewards been consistently delivered? Have they been given immediately? Have you been praising your child and putting effort into the program? You need to be very honest with yourself about the answers to these questions. If you are not consistent and do not support and reward your child as promised, you cannot expect him or her to take the program seriously. If this is the case, it is never too late to get back on track.

It is sometimes the case that children just run out of steam with the process of stepladders and get bored with the same old rewards that are being offered. The initial excitement that often comes with starting a new activity, picking rewards, and working on something together might just have worn off for the moment. If this is the case, it is often possible to get your child moving again with a bit of a reward kick start. Discuss the rewards you have set for each step with your child and see whether there are any that he or she might want to change. Perhaps setting the next one or two rewards as slightly bigger ones might provide the motivation needed to get your child going again.

Finally, you need to ask yourself whether you might have some worries about how much to push your child to try something a bit harder. Often there may be a "soft" and a "hard" parent, disagreement between you as parents, or one parent opting out of the treatment plan, all of which can reduce your child's enthusiasm. Try to talk these issues over and agree on a joint strategy to help your child. If you are finding it hard to be "tough" and push your child, you may need to try some of the realistic thinking on your own worries. As long as you continue to show your child that you love him or her, some pushing will not cause your child to hate you or to become mentally scarred or damaged. Remember that being a little tough now will help your child become more confident in the long run.

Need for Reassurance

We discussed the issue of reassurance seeking in chapter 4. While seeking excessive reassurance can be a problem in many areas of an anxious child's life, it may become especially apparent during stepladders. When you do stepladders, you may find that your child constantly asks questions such as, "What is going to happen?" "Exactly what time will you be back?" and "Will you be okay?" Being a loving parent, it is very hard to ignore these requests for reassurance. But it is very important not to give in by providing too much reassurance for your child during stepladders. This does not mean that you need to be nasty or hard, but rather that you gradually need to encourage your child to rely more and more on his or her own judgment. If seeking reassurance is a particular problem for your child, you may need to try and include it in the stepladder. For example, you may encourage your child to sleep at a friend's house as one step, allowing some reassurance questions, and then the next step might repeat the process but without allowing any questioning. It may be a good idea to go back to chapter 4 to reread the section "Ignoring Behaviors That You Don't Want."

LASHI'S EXAMPLE

Lashi had been working on one of her stepladders for going to sleep in her own bed with the light off. She was doing very well, was finally able to sleep in her own bed all night, and was allowing her mother to turn off all the lights in her part of the house. But there was still an anxious habit that needed to be addressed. Every night when Lashi went to bed, she would call her mother to her room four or five times before she finally went to sleep. At these times, Lashi would ask a bunch of questions such as, "Are you staying home tonight?" "Have you checked the doors and windows?" and "How long will you be up?" Lashi's mother was answering all of these questions because she was so pleased with Lashi's progress. But she soon realized that she was going to have to work on this reassurance seeking because it was stopping Lashi from becoming self-confident. Lashi and her mother discussed how they could include these questions in Lashi's stepladder. They decided that at first, Lashi could call her mother into her room twice before she went to sleep. After that, her mother would ignore her. At the next step, Lashi could only call her mother into her room once after going to bed. Then Lashi and her mother would go through Lashi's realistic thinking before Lashi went to bed, but she could not call her mother after going to bed. Finally, Lashi was rewarded only for going to bed without any reassurance from her mother either before or after going to bed.

Dealing with "Failure"

Anxious children seem to have more sensitive "failure" detectors than other children, so the importance of a minor setback in doing a simple task will be greatly magnified in their eyes. This can be a blow to their confidence and may increase the level of anxiety about attempting any further steps or even things they found quite easy to do before. Many anxious children easily slip into negative self-talk such as, "I'm hopeless; I knew I couldn't do anything right."

If your child tries one of his or her steps and suddenly finds that it is too hard, or is not able to do it all as planned, he or she may see this as a complete failure. If this happens, it's important to encourage your child to do some detective thinking about the importance of the success or failure of these efforts. Role reversal is a particularly good source of evidence to use. In other words, ask children to imagine what they would say to someone else who was in the same position. Try to point out that there is no real failure in doing stepladders. Each attempt is an opportunity to learn. If they were not able to do that step, it simply means that the step was too hard and they need to break it down into smaller, easier steps.

On the other hand, some anxious children actually get worried about being successful because then they might have to do even better next time. In other words, for some kids, doing a good job makes them feel under more pressure for next time. If this is true for your child, you may find that he or she plays down or even completely denies his or her successes. This tends to happen with very perfectionistic children, in particular.

You will need to stress to your child that doing stepladders is what counts—not winning or being the best. Again, remind your child that there is no way to fail stepladders—he or she just needs to do it. You may also want to include some stepladder exercises aimed at reducing any perfectionism.

Taking On Too Much

A different sort of problem arises if your child is trying really hard to please you and to be the "perfect child." In this case, you may find that your child will choose stepladder steps that are just too hard. Sometimes it is so easy for you to get caught up in the excitement that you begin to encourage your child to take on harder and harder steps and might begin to go a bit too quickly.

It is important to praise your child for his or her enthusiasm. Having a child who wants to try hard is wonderful. But you also need to remind your child that everyone is individual and that there are no prizes for being the first to finish. If the steps are too big, your child is more likely not to be able to do them and may then begin to lose confidence. Go back to your list and make sure that the big steps are broken down into more manageable and easier steps.

Speeding Through

In some cases children can have a sort of breakthrough—in other words, by facing one or two situations that they may have avoided for years, they get a sudden burst of confidence and lose their fears very quickly. If this happens, it can be wonderful.

However, for other children, moving too quickly through the steps may be a sign that they are not learning anything from the stepladders. On the one hand, it may mean that the steps are just not challenging enough for your child. If this is the case, you will need to sit down together and come up with some more difficult steps. On the other hand, the steps may be so difficult that your child is not willing to stay in the situation long enough to learn that nothing bad will happen. Or it may be that your child is "cheating" a little and not fully engaging in each step. If this is the case, you simply need to encourage your child to redo the steps but include more detail in the instructions you give. For example, you may need to specify how long your child stays in the situation or teach him or her such things as where to sit and how much to say.

GEORGE'S EXAMPLE

One of George's big fears was going to parties and having to mix socially with other kids. After doing stepladders for a while and gradually building his confidence, an opportunity came up when he was invited to a party at a friend's house. Even though this was pretty scary for George, his parents encouraged him to put it on his stepladder and give it a try. When George came home after the party, his father asked him how it went. "Fine" was all he said. Something in his tone made his father think that it all seemed too easy. So he asked George to sit down and tell him exactly what he had done at the party. George looked sheepish and admitted that he had gone to the party as they agreed but had spent the entire evening sitting in a corner watching everyone. George got his reward, as agreed, for going to the party, but his parents suggested that next time he would need to make sure he mixed with some of the kids. When the next party came up, the step was not only to go to the party, but to make sure that George spoke with at least three different kids while there. This time when he got home, George said that it had been pretty hard but he was also surprised at how much he had in common with one kid there and they had actually gotten along quite well.

Ups and Downs

During the stepladders process, there will be some days that seem better than others and progress will not always be smooth. You should act as a coach to encourage your child to do the best he or she can do on any given day and to keep trying the next day. On bad days, it may be better to repeat a step already achieved than to try a new, more difficult step. Rewarding good attempts as well as success at achieving the step will encourage your child's ability to persist and to tolerate what he or she sees as failure.

Worried Sick

Most parents and therapists would agree that anxious children and adolescents "wrote the book" when it comes to excuses and explanations about why they can't do something. A common, and sometimes the most difficult, problem for parents to deal with is complaints of illness at times of stress. Headaches, sore stomachs, and "feeling sick" are difficult to deal with when you are not sure of the cause. And sometimes parents or caregivers disagree with each other about the reason for the complaints.

Consultation with the family doctor may be necessary as a first step to exclude physical problems. This is important if there is disagreement between you and your child's other primary caregiver over the cause of the complaints and the most appropriate way to manage them. It is important that there is a consistent approach taken by everyone involved. In families where the parents are divorced and the child moves between two households, these issues will need the involvement and agreement of all the adults involved in the child's care. This can include the schoolteacher and school nurse.

In families with a history of physical illness, where there may be strong anxieties about physical pain, those worries will need to be dealt with first. If this applies to your family, you may need to work through your concerns about this issue. Try to use your realistic thinking about your own concerns about your child's health. Look at the realistic consequences of both encouraging your child to challenge his or her fears and of allowing the avoidance to continue and perhaps worsen.

LASHI'S EXAMPLE

As Lashi moved through the program, Lashi's mother decided that it was time that she started to go out and leave Lashi at home with a sitter. On the first night that she was getting ready to go out, Lashi began to cry and throw a huge tantrum. She became so worked up that she vomited. Lashi's mother ended up canceling the sitter and staying home. After that, Lashi began to complain of stomachaches and feeling sick every time her mother wanted to go anywhere and even on some days when she had to go to school. Sometimes, Lashi got so worked up that she would, again, make herself physically sick.

As a first step, Lashi's mother took her to the doctor to get a full checkup. "All clear" was the doctor's diagnosis—"This is a healthy little girl." After that, Lashi's mother told her that when they worked on the stepladder, they would do whatever they had agreed on whether or not Lashi felt sick. Lashi's mother contacted the school, and they agreed that if Lashi felt sick at school, she could go to the nurse and rest for a while and then she would go back to class—Lashi's mother would not come and pick her up unless she had a fever.

Soon after, Lashi's mother was asked to a party. Lashi and her mother discussed the situation and decided that this was a reasonable step for the stepladder. However, on the night of the party, Lashi began to feel sick and have pains. Lashi's mother told her that she understood how hard it all was and that she really felt bad about her pain, but that she was going to go to the party anyway. She gave the sitter detailed instructions about how to handle Lashi and to call her only if Lashi had a fever. That night was hard for both Lashi and her mom, but in the morning Lashi got a big reward for doing her step from the stepladder. Lashi's mom went out on two more occasions with the same results. It was not easy, but they both stuck with it.

Finally, on the fourth time, Lashi was not sick when her mom went out. Even though she was still scared, she did not throw up and did not complain of stomachaches. To celebrate, Lashi got an extra reward in the morning.

Smart Tricks

People can reduce their fear by using superstitious behaviors such as carrying a lucky charm or special toy, wearing certain lucky clothes, humming a song, chewing gum, or going through a particular ritual before doing something that causes anxiety. All these methods of avoidance are used by adults, including sports stars and actors, and they are often used by anxious children.

These beliefs and behaviors can act as subtle ways of avoiding facing up to the feared situation. If your child uses any of these subtle types of avoidance, the big risk is that he or she may not believe that a success is due to his or her own ability. Instead, your child may attribute success to the special object or ritual.

To properly overcome anxiety, your child needs to experience the fear, use the realistic thinking techniques to realistically assess the level of danger, and then experience the situation to learn that there was no need for that level of concern. Your child must be able to attribute his or her subsequent lack of fear to a real lack of danger, not to the magical protective powers of a lucky charm, a crystal, or special socks.

Children with separation fears are increasingly reliant upon having instant access to their parents (for example, via the mobile cell phone), and this is a subtle type of avoidance. You may find that your own anxieties can play a part in this overreliance on immediate contact as well. Look carefully at the line between safety issues and the convenience of being in reasonable contact with each other, on the one hand, and a subtle avoidance of dealing with fears about separation, on the other.

Safety strategies and superstitious behaviors are especially common in children with obsessive-compulsive fears. These children have often developed very subtle rituals and magical ways of doing things that they might believe can protect them from danger. For example, your child might count to a magic number under his or her breath, might touch things in a particular way, or might move in a certain pattern. These things may be very hard to see, and as a result you will probably not be aware of all the rituals that your child does. It is important to regularly ask your child about these types of activities. The best question is to ask your child after every step of the stepladder, "Is there anything you could have done differently that would have made it harder?" Make sure that doing the activity without the rituals is part of the stepladder.

A special example of subtle avoidance might be found in children who are taking medication for their anxiety. If your child is on anti-anxiety medication while doing stepladders, it is very possible that he or she will think, "The only reason I could do that was because my medication helped me through it." In this case, your child will not be building his or her own confidence but instead will be learning that he or she can only cope with the help of a drug.

The existence of lucky charms, aids, or medication is not a major problem. It simply means that the stepladder steps will need to be repeated at some point without these things. In the case of charms or other aids, you can actually organize the steps so that they are each done the first time with the aid and then repeated without it. In the case of medication, your child may need to complete all or most of his or her anxiety program while taking the medication. Then, when improvements seem to be going very well, you may want to begin to reduce the medication under the guidance of the prescribing physician. Once the medication has been stopped, you will need to go through a few of the stepladder steps again, just to convince your child that it really is him or her who is in control.

TALIA'S EXAMPLE

Talia had been working on her stepladder of going swimming for some time and was getting really confident in the water. Talia's dad really wanted to be involved and had taken a very active part in the whole process. As part of his involvement, Talia's father had been going with her to all of the steps of her stepladder. Each time Talia went into the water, her dad would stand outside and watch her. Talia regularly waved to her dad and would look at him a lot. On one occasion, Talia was at the beach swimming and having a great time. Her dad decided to go off to get an ice-cream. When he returned, Talia was out of the water and crying. She screamed at him, "Where did you go? I might have drowned!" Talia's father suddenly realized that by being with her for all of her steps, Talia had learned to use him as a safety cue. As a result, Talia could only face deep water when he was around. Talia and her dad discussed the problem and decided that she needed to start over and redo most of her stepladder but this time without her dad being there. Going through the stepladder the second time was much faster, and it wasn't long before Talia's confidence in the water was sky high.

PARENT ACTIVITY: REVIEWING EARLY ATTEMPTS AT FACING FEARS

Looking at your records of your child facing fears, list the successes he or she has had.

_____

_____

What rewards did your child receive for these successes?

_____

_____

What rewards did your child receive for putting in effort on the not-so-successful attempts?

_____

What types of problems did your child have in completing their steps?

_____

_____

What could you do to overcome these problems?

_____

_____

_____

Could you see any behaviors, magical objects, or ways of doing things that your child might have used to help him or her get through the activity? Did you ask your child what could have made the situation more frightening?

_____

_____

_____

OBSTACLES TO YOUR CHILD'S PROGRESS

In addition to difficulties that your child may face when attempting to manage anxiety or when working on steps, there are also other difficulties that could undermine your child's progress. Some of the possible obstacles are discussed below.

Not Enough Time for Stepladders

Insufficient time is a very common problem because most family members have very busy lives. Continuing improvement will require the prioritizing of stepladders, detective thinking, and other new skills so they can be structured into your and your child's life. Eventually the time required for consistent practice will decrease. Remember, the more practice there is, the more the skills will be used naturally in other areas of life. Your child will experience less anxiety and he or she will be able to use anxiety management skills independently.

Limited Parent Motivation to Create Opportunities for Steps

To maintain motivation for anything, we need to provide ourselves with incentives to keep going. You need to reward yourself for your efforts in helping your child manage his or her anxiety. Reviewing your child's records about the successes he or she is having can help maintain your motivation. Success increases motivation; you may need to remind yourself of the small successes that will eventually make up the big success that your child is working toward. You may want to look back at "Children's Activity 4: My Goals" in chapter 1 to remind yourself (and your child) of the changes your child is aiming for. Your motivation may also increase if you use the anxiety management strategies to address any of your own unrealistic anxieties, if relevant, because you will get firsthand experience of the positive effect of the practice.

Knowing When to Push (Anxiety Versus Disinterest)

Knowing when to push will involve trusting what your child is telling you. Older children will often be able to tell you when their refusal to do a task or enter a situation is due to anxiety or disinterest, but you may need to ask them. But sometimes children will say that they aren't interested in something when they are really stopped by fear. For example, a child who is invited to a party where there are other kids he or she doesn't know well, might say that the party will be boring or uncool, when really it is worry that is getting in the way. You will need to think carefully about whether your child really isn't interested in these things or is simply anxious. Your child may have particular cues that are familiar to you that tell you when he or she is feeling anxious and worried or simply disinterested. Get to know these cues to help you distinguish between anxiety and disinterest. You may find it useful to look at the cues you discovered in the first weeks of the program. If you do find that reluctance to do a task or enter a situation is due to anxiety, try to problem solve what might be getting in the way (for example, the steps may be too big). Remember to reward your child when you are gently pushing him or her, and combine steps with rewards regularly. Finally, if you are not sure whether your child is anxious or really is bored with doing something, it may be best to challenge your child to do it anyway. Tell your child that if he or she is bored with the step, this will be the easiest way ever to have earned a reward.

Taking Over Because It Is Easier or Faster

There will be times when you are tempted to take over. Try not to give in to this temptation! Children need a clear and consistent message that it is okay for them to face their fears and that they can do so independently. Remember that when your child does something that is close to what you want, this should be praised or rewarded too.

Parent Anxiety Getting in the Way of Facing Fears

At times parents find that their own unrealistic anxiety gets in the way of allowing their children to participate in stepladders or other everyday activities. You could try to apply, for yourself, the anxiety management strategies that you have taught your child, or you may choose to seek professional assistance. Modeling your own efforts to face your own fears will be a powerful message to your child that he or she can also manage anxiety.

One of the biggest difficulties for anxious parents will be trying to decide what is a reasonable thing for their children to do alone and what is really dangerous. For example, should you let your child walk home from school, stay home alone, go to that party, and so on? This is a time when getting feedback from other parents can be really useful. Talk to other parents whose children are in the same situation and get their opinion. And don't forget to do your realistic thinking—look for evidence about what sorts of things could realistically go wrong.

Parent Beliefs or Expectations Getting in the Way

Your own beliefs and expectations about different situations can be difficult to recognize because often they have been around for a very long time and they influence what you do without you thinking about it. A simple example of how a belief influences the way we behave would be that we automatically make coffee each morning because we believe that we won't be able to function without it. Your beliefs and expectations can influence your child's progress. For example, if a parent believes that authority figures are "superior," he or she may not expect a child, who gets anxious when speaking to the principal, to face this fear. Similarly, a parent may expect a child to be "perfect" at particular tasks such as schoolwork or sports because that parent believes that when his or her child makes a mistake, it reflects negatively on the child and on his or her parenting ability. This parent might not want his or her child to make mistakes as part of a stepladder that aims to reduce the child's need for perfection.

Being aware of such beliefs or expectations is the first step to reducing their impact on your child's progress. Try to problem solve ways to reduce the influence of your beliefs and expectations on your child, such as doing your own realistic thinking about that belief or, if your child's fear also reflects a fear of your own, doing the stepladder tasks with your child. If you feel that your beliefs or expectations are a significant obstacle to your child's progress and it is too difficult to manage independently, it is worth seeking help from a professional who can work through the issues with you.

ACTIVITIES TO DO WITH YOUR CHILD …

CHILDREN'S ACTIVITY 24: WHEN THE GOING GETS TOUGH

Talk with your child about the common difficulties that can occur when facing fears. These include steps that are too hard or too easy, steps that haven't been described well, having really worried thoughts when facing a step, not staying in a situation long enough for fear to start declining, moving on to the next step before the previous one was mastered, forgetting where you are on the stepladder, not giving yourself rewards, and using tricks to reduce the amount of worry experienced during the step (such as listening to music or going somewhere, but only with a friend). Help your child to identify possible solutions to these problems in the following ways:

- Use coping skills in preparation for each step.

- Be persistent and do a lot of practice.

- Keep records (as much to make sure that you follow through with rewards as anything else).

- Do each step until it is, or nearly is, boring.

- Revise steps so that they always feel challenging but not impossible.

CHILDREN'S PRACTICE TASK 6: DOING STEPS

Once again, work with your child to create written plans on what steps will be attempted in the coming week(s). Also remind your child to use his or her cue cards during steps and, when needed, to use detective thinking and problem solving as ways of managing anxiety.

CHAPTER HIGHLIGHTS

In this chapter, you learned ...

- Possible solutions to some of the common difficulties that can be faced when working through stepladders include the following:

    - Revising the stepladders and rethinking rewards when you get stuck

    - Reducing reassurance to ensure children learn they can cope alone

    - Using detective thinking to deal with "failed" steps

    - Making sure steps are not too big or too small

    - Accepting that there will be good days and bad days

    - Persisting despite physical symptoms of illnesses

    - Being vigilant about finding safety strategies that children may be using to reduce the anxiety that they experience during steps

- Some of the obstacles that can interfere with progress include the following:

    - Not dedicating enough time to working on stepladders

    - Not providing enough opportunities to do steps

    - Being unsure of when to push your child to try the next step

    - Taking over because it is easier

    - Demotivating children with parents' own anxieties or beliefs

Your child will need to do the following:

- Complete the children's activity with the help of a parent or other adult.

- Continue to work on steps from his or her stepladders, using other anxiety management skills to help with any fears or worries that arise. (By now you should really be encouraging your child to move on and up those steps.)

CHAPTER 8

Assertiveness and Social Skills

THE IMPORTANCE OF SOCIAL SKILLS

Most anxious children are perfectly competent at making friends and interacting with other people. However, some anxious children simply don't seem to be able to interact with others in a smooth or skilled manner. Sometimes this can make other children and even adults react negatively to these children by ignoring them, rejecting them, or even teasing them. As you can imagine, if this happens, it makes it pretty hard for an already anxious child to learn to be more confident.

George's Example

George spends most of his spare time alone. Even at school, you will find him on his own. He rarely speaks to his classmates. At lunchtime, he usually goes to the library and sits on his own, reading a book. Sometimes he walks around the school and stops to watch some of his classmates playing soccer. They never ask him to join in. In fact, they don't notice that he is there. George would love to join in, but he can't think of how to ask and he is afraid that they will laugh at him or refuse to let him play. He returns to the classroom after lunch and sits at the back of the class hoping not to be called upon to answer any questions. He doesn't speak to the other students. He really likes the girl who sits in front of him in science class. He would love to talk to her but he can't think of what to say and is afraid that he would get it wrong and feel stupid. The class teacher is going around the class asking everyone to give an idea for the school festival. George thinks it would be a good idea to run a coconut stall where you win a prize for knocking the coconut off a stand. George's turn comes. He looks down at his desk and mumbles, wishing that he could disappear. He tries to explain his idea to the teacher, but his voice is too quiet and no one can hear him. The teacher moves on to the next person in the class.

After school, George walks home on his own. One of his classmates goes the same way home. George notices that the boy has dropped his school folder and the pages are flying around. George wants to offer to help but is not sure what to say. He walks past, leaving the boy to pick up the papers on his own.

The next day, George is standing in line at the school cafeteria, waiting to buy some lunch. Another boy pushes in front of him, leaving George feeling angry. He would love to tell the boy to go back to the end of the line but he does not say anything.

Why Are Social Skills and Assertiveness Important?

Children need to be successful in a wide range of situations with other children and with adults, including parents and teachers. For example, with other children, they need to be able to hold conversations, ask to join in games or activities, and invite other children to play or to come over for a visit. They need to be able to ask questions, ask to take a turn in a game, give compliments, offer toys or items to other children, and assert their rights if they are unfairly treated. All these activities are important if children are to make friends and be accepted into their peer group.

Children also need to be able to handle adults. For example, they need to be able to ask for help when they need it, offer to help, express their point of view, pick the right moment to interrupt, answer questions, and start and maintain conversations with adults. When you start to think about it, there are an enormous number of social tasks that children have to be able to perform in a competent way. By the time children reach adolescence, there are an even greater number of social situations that they have to learn to handle, including romantic relationships, getting through job interviews, and keeping a job.

The skills that we need in order to perform these social tasks successfully are called *social skills*. Our research shows that some anxious children perform more poorly than other children on many social tasks. There are two possibilities as to why this might be the case. It might be that some anxious children are too afraid to use their skills. In other words, they might know what to do, but their anxiety stops them from doing it. Alternatively, some anxious children may not develop their social skills because they have less experience and practice at interacting with other children. Many anxious children avoid interactions with others and therefore may have less opportunity to practice how to interact with other people. Whatever the explanation, our research has shown that there are significant benefits to teaching anxious children social skills in order to improve their relationships with others. Anxious children also tend not to be very assertive. Assertiveness is the ability to express your needs, to assert your rights with other people, and to stick up for yourself in a way that produces a positive outcome.

THE SOCIAL SKILLS HIERARCHY

There are five main areas of social skills; these skills are generally progressive, with the skills listed first being needed before the latter skills can develop.

Body Language Skills

Eye contact: Child looks others in the eye during conversations to show that he or she is listening and paying attention but does not stare excessively.

Many anxious children avoid making eye contact and tend to look down or away when talking to others. This may be seen by others as indicating unfriendliness and lack of interest. It's also a problem if children make too much eye contact during conversations and stare at others too much, as this makes other people feel uncomfortable.

Posture: Child sits or stands in a way that's appropriate for the situation.

Some postures, such as being slumped, hunched up, turning away from the other person, or being excessively rigid and upright, may create a poor impression on others.

Facial expression: Child's facial expressions are appropriate to the situation. He or she smiles and has a friendly face when talking generally with others and uses sad and angry facial expressions occasionally, appropriate to the situation.

Facial expressions communicate how we are feeling. Bored, angry, or fearful facial expressions or lack of smiling may be seen by other children and adults as a sign of unfriendliness.

Voice-Quality Skills

Tone and pitch: Child's speech is usually friendly, expressive, and pleasant to listen to. The child can use different tones of voice to communicate different emotions.

If a child's voice sounds boring, aggressive, fearful, whining, or is unpleasant to listen to, then this may lead to misunderstandings with other people who may misinterpret the tone of voice, thinking the child unfriendly, aggressive, or uninterested. Children need to be able to use a friendly tone of voice in most situations.

Volume: Child's volume of speech is appropriate for different situations.

Children need to be able to speak up so that they're heard and yet not to speak so loud as to be inappropriate. Many anxious children speak too quietly, which interferes with their communication with others.

Rate: Child speaks at an appropriate rate—not too quickly and not too slowly.

Very slow speech may sound boring. Very fast speech is hard to follow.

Clarity: Child speaks clearly and is easy to understand.

Conversations are difficult if children's speech is hard to follow. Some anxious children tend to mumble and have difficulty speaking clearly enough that others can understand them.

Conversation Skills

Greetings and introductions: Child says "hello" or other greeting when meeting people he or she knows. For older children, the ability to introduce themselves to others is important.

Most children know what to say when they greet someone but they may be too anxious to do so or they may not do so in a socially skilled way. In all conversation skills, children must remember to use the basic skills of eye contact, appropriate facial expression, and clear, audible speech.

Starting conversations: Child is able to start a conversation by asking simple questions or making simple statements.

Some anxious children avoid starting conversations with others. They tend to be quiet most of the time, particularly with people they don't know well. This makes it difficult for them to form friendships with other children.

Holding conversations—answering questions: Child listens to what the other person has said and answers with some detail rather than with very brief answers.

Some anxious children give very short answers when other people ask them a question. The information that they give is minimal and does not convey the message that he or she would like to continue the conversation or is interested in the other person.

Holding conversations—asking questions: Child asks appropriate questions of the other person to allow the conversation to continue. The questions are likely to be of interest to the other person.

Children need to be able to ask questions in order to continue a conversation. Not asking questions often gives the impression that they are not interested and don't want to mix with the other person.

Holding conversations—taking turns: Child takes turns in conversations, listens to others, and then returns with an appropriate comment or question.

Two-way conversation skills are important if children are going to form friendships. Sometimes anxious children tend to interrupt or talk over the top of others in their attempts to get their answers out at all costs.

Choosing topics of conversation: Child picks appropriate topics of conversation.

It is important that children can pick conversation topics that the other person is interested in and that are appropriate to the situation. Anxious children often have difficulty thinking of things to talk about. They need to learn about the types of things that other children are interested in if they are going to form friendships.

Using polite conversation: Child uses polite speech and says "please" and "thank you" as appropriate.

For most children this is not a problem, but we mention it because the rules of polite communication are an important factor in determining the impression that children make upon adults (e.g., teachers) and peers.

Friendship Skills

Offering help or items: Child offers to help other children or adults, or offers to lend or give items where appropriate.

Forming friendships requires that children can show kindness to others. One part of this is to be able to offer to help others when they need it. Friendship involves giving and receiving help of various kinds. Some anxious children will stand by and do nothing when they really want to help. This may then be misinterpreted as unfriendliness and lack of caring.

Offering invitations: Child invites other children to join in with activities or to come over to his or her house.

Friendships involve spending time together and making an effort by showing that you would like to make friends. Offering invitations to others and initiating activities is part of this process.

Asking to join in: Child approaches other children to ask to join in their activity.

Many anxious children are reluctant to ask other children if they can join in their activity. Often they really want to join in, but they stand on the edge of the activity watching because they may not know what to say or may be too afraid to try for fear of looking foolish.

Expressing affection: Child expresses affection toward children and adults where appropriate, either using speech or physical gestures such as holding hands, hugs, gentle touches, and pats on the back.

The ability to show affection is important in forming friendships with peers. This can be something very simple and physical and does not have to be verbal.

Giving compliments: Child gives compliments to others (adults and children) when appropriate.

The ability to give positive feedback to other people is an important part of friendship. It shows that one person is interested in the other and wants to make that person feel good. This is just as important in children's friendships as it is in adult relationships.

Showing caring when others are hurt or upset: Child tries to help others and to care for them when they are hurt or upset.

Children need to be sensitive to other people and to show that they care when others are hurt or upset. Children cannot always do something to help, but they may try to check that the other person is okay and try to comfort that person in some way, which might be physical (e.g., a gentle touch), a spoken comment, or by asking someone else to help.

Assertiveness Skills

Sticking up for one's rights: Child is able to stick up for his or her rights without causing harm to other people.

There are many situations in which children have to learn how to stick up for themselves. There will be times when other children or adults try to take advantage of them, do not attend to their needs, or try to pressure them into doing something that they don't want to do. Anxious children tend to be unassertive and have difficulty sticking up for their rights. However, if children are too active in asserting themselves, then this may become aggression. In all instances, it is important that children deal with these situations in a way that does not cause harm to other people. Assertiveness requires communication of clear messages, in a loud, strong voice (but not an aggressive one). It requires being able to say how one feels and exactly what one does or does not want to happen. If a problem is too difficult to solve, the child may need to actively seek help from an adult.

Asking for help or information or expressing needs: Child is able to ask for help or information and to inform others when he or she needs something.

At school, it is particularly important that children can ask for help, clarification, or information from their teachers when they need it. Problems may arise if children remain silent when they need help. Children also need to be able to request help from their peers.

Saying no: Child is able to refuse unreasonable requests and to say no when he or she wishes to do so.

It is important that children are able to say when they don't want to do something. They need to be able to say how they feel and to refuse unreasonable requests from others. Some children may find themselves doing things that they don't want to do or having things taken from them because they have not clearly stated how they feel or clearly communicated the answer "no."

Dealing with teasing: Child is able to deal successfully with teasing from others.

All children have to deal with teasing. They need to be able to put a stop to excessive teasing and to learn not to become too hurt by it. Of course, if it is very frequent and severe, you and your school will need to become involved.

Dealing with bullying: Child is able to stop attempts at bullying by others, either by using his or her own strategies or by seeking the help of others.

As with teasing, all children will encounter incidents of bullying at some point in their lives. However, no child should have to put up with bullying, and we will discuss various ways in which children can put a stop to it. Again, parents and schools need to become involved in ongoing cases.

PARENT ACTIVITY:
MY CHILD'S SOCIAL SKILLS

Not all children have problems with social skills. Observe your child carefully over one week and evaluate his or her performance. Performance does not need to be perfect, but make a note if you think lack of a skill is causing problems in his or her relationships with others. Remember the social skills that children use are different from the ones that we use as adults. Try to think about whether your child's skills seem comparable with those of other children his or her age. It may also be helpful to talk to teachers about skill level, with peers and in class, as this may differ significantly from home.

Which of the following social skills did you identify as needing work for your child?

Body Language

- Eye contact
- Posture
- Facial expression

Voice Quality

- Tone and pitch
- Volume
- Rate
- Clarity

Conversation Skills

- Greetings and Introductions
- Starting conversations
- Holding conversations
  —Answering questions
  —Asking questions
  —Taking turns
- Choosing topics of conversation
- Using polite conversation

Friendship Skills

- Offering help or items
- Offering invitations
- Asking to join in
- Expressing affection
- Giving compliments
- Showing caring when others are hurt or upset

Assertiveness

- Sticking up for one's rights
- Asking for help or information or expressing needs
- Saying no
- Dealing with teasing
- Dealing with bullying

TEACHING SOCIAL SKILLS

There are many ways in which you can teach social skills to your child. The strategies that you use for teaching will depend on how much difficulty your child has in using social skills. Some children have just a few areas of difficulty. Others may have poor performance in many of the skills described in "The Social Skills Hierarchy" section above. For those children who have just a few areas of difficulty, we use a strategy called *incidental teaching*.

Incidental Teaching

Incidental teaching involves using opportunities that occur in everyday life to teach a particular skill rather than having special teaching sessions that are dedicated to training your child to use social skills. Incidental teaching involves the following:

- Identifying social situations in which particular social skills are needed

- Explaining to your child that a particular skill is needed in that situation and how it should be performed

- Explaining why it is important

- Checking that your child has understood what is needed

- Prompting your child to use the skill

- Praising your child for attempting to use the skill and describing what he or she did well

- Giving your child gentle feedback about ways in which the skill could be improved

When you are using incidental teaching, it is important that you keep things really simple and stick to one skill at a time. Children become confused if they have to concentrate on too many things at once. When an appropriate situation arises, decide which skill is most important. Make sure that the skill is not too difficult and that your child has learned simpler skills first. Incidental teaching of social skills can easily be included in your child's stepladders.

JESS'S EXAMPLE

Jess's parents noticed that she rarely made eye contact with other children or with her teachers. Jess tended to look down or away when other people spoke to her. Jess and her father had to attend a parent-teacher evening at the school. Her father suggested that Jess work on making eye contact with her teacher during the interview. Jess and her father discussed why it was important to make eye contact and how this influenced the impression that people make on each other. Jess understood what was required and laughed when she found herself making eye contact with her father. Just before going into the classroom for their interview, Jess's father prompted his daughter to remind her to use eye contact with the teacher. During the interview Jess tried hard, and her father noticed Jess making occasional eye contact with the teacher. Once they were alone again, her father told Jess how well she had done and how he had noticed the big improvement. They talked about how it had felt and about other situations in which eye contact would be important.

Helping Children Who Need More Intensive Teaching

Some children will need more intensive teaching in order to learn to be more socially skilled. Here are some guidelines about how to teach social skills to your child using a more structured approach. The teaching methods are basically the same as for incidental teaching. For each skill, you will be using the following teaching methods:

- Instruction and explanation

- Practice and prompting of the skill

- Feedback

- Praise

Social skills are like building blocks. Often it is difficult to know which skills to teach and where to start. We believe that children need to work on each small skill and then gradually put them all together to create a good performance. We suggest that you start with body language skills and when your child is good at these, move on to conversation skills.

When you are teaching social skills to your child, he or she may feel a bit uncomfortable and embarrassed, so it is helpful to use games and enjoyable activities. Humor is also a good way of reducing anxiety and making the sessions enjoyable. However, it is important to laugh with your child and not at your child.

GIVING INSTRUCTIONS

Ideally you should focus on just one skill at a time, and that skill becomes the theme of the session. When you teach a skill to a child, you need to begin by giving information about the skill. In particular, you need to give information about the following:

- Exactly what is involved in the skill—how is it performed?

- Why is it important—what happens if the skill is not used?

Having discussed the skill, it is important to then demonstrate how the skill is performed. You can regard yourself as a bit like a coach in a sports situation. You can demonstrate the skill yourself or find some real-life examples to show your child. For example, you could watch other people in a shopping center or on television and discuss how they are using the skill.

It often works well to show what happens when the skill is *not* used. This can produce some comical situations. For example, you can hold a conversation with your child without using any eye contact.

You can then discuss why eye contact is important and how your child felt while you were doing this. Another activity might be to sit in a café together and look for people who don't use social skills well. A fun idea, especially with younger children, is to watch their favorite television show with them and see who can pick out examples of good and bad skills the quickest.

The instructions phase is more difficult with younger children. It basically consists of giving prompts or requests for use of the skill (for example, "I am going to ask you a question, and when you give your answer, I want you to use a loud, clear voice so that I can hear what you say. Can we try that now?"). With younger children, you can also demonstrate skills by using puppets (for example, two puppets can be used to show how to say "hello" and ask questions of each other). You can also use puppets to demonstrate appropriate eye contact and voice volume. Keep asking your child what he or she thinks of the puppet that didn't use the skill and how he or she would react to that puppet.

Often the main problem is that children simply do not realize how they are coming across to others. The more you can get them to experience what it is like to interact with someone who has poor skills, the better. Pointing out that children who do not use social skills very well also tend to be less popular, and that learning to use these skills well will help in making friends, may help to motivate your child.

PRACTICING BODY LANGUAGE AND CONVERSATION SKILLS

Once you have explained to your child how a skill should be performed and the possible downsides of not using it, it's time to start to practice using the skill. To begin with, it is best to practice in the safety of your home where things can't go too wrong. And in the same way that you need to practice hitting a tennis ball in order to become a good tennis player, progress in social skills will only be made with regular practice. Ideally, your child should practice every day.

In the teaching of the simpler social skills, such as body language or conversation skills, we suggest that you practice using short conversations together. One fun way to do this is to develop a set of practice cue cards. Conversation topics are written onto the cue cards and prompt a short talk between you and your child during which each skill can be practiced. For example, one time you might use the cue cards to work on eye contact—your child would pick a card from the top of the pile and start a short conversation with you while making sure he or she kept good eye contact. On a different occasion, your child might pick another card and this time focus on increasing voice volume.

Here are some examples of cue cards that you might find useful:

- What is your favorite movie? ... Now tell me what the film was about.

- What is your favorite book? ... Now tell me all about the story in the book.

- Tell me about your favorite hobby.

- Pick someone in your family. What exactly does this person look like?

- Tell me about what you did last weekend.

- What is your favorite TV show? Explain to me why you like it.

- Ask me some questions about when I was a child.

- Ask me about people in my family.

- Ask me about where I would like to go for a holiday.

When you are teaching a new skill, it is important to stick to one skill at a time. Only move on to teaching the next skill once your child is able to perform the first one reasonably well. When you do move on to a new skill, you need to keep prompting your child to remember to use the body language and voice skills that he or she has already learned. For example, when you are teaching your child to ask questions, here are some prompts you can give: "Pick a sensible topic, make clear eye contact, use a friendly facial expression, and ask your question in a clear, loud voice."

Also, spend some time talking with your child about how to choose appropriate topics for starting up a conversation. For example, topics might include a TV program, a sports team, the local news, movies, pets, hobbies, or asking about other people (e.g., their health, their opinion, their favorite activity). Together with your child, you might like to make a list of topics that children at school tend to talk about in their free time.

When your child has learned the basics of body language and conversation skills, you can move on to teach more complicated social skills relating to making friends and assertiveness. In addition to the teaching methods that we have already described, there are two additional techniques for coaching your child in more complex social skills. These teaching methods involve problem solving and role-play.

PROBLEM SOLVING

Problem solving involves brainstorming as many solutions to a problem as possible and then choosing solutions or combinations of solutions that are most likely to work. Brainstorming can be great fun. For any particular social problem, there are many possible solutions. When you brainstorm with your child, you do not need to worry about how silly or successful different ideas are likely to be. The aim is get as many different responses as possible.

For example, imagine a situation in which your child is unfairly accused by the teacher of talking in class when he or she did not do this. Together with your child, you make a list of the possible actions that your child could take. Here is one list of possibilities that you might produce:

- Shout at the teacher that you did not do it.

- Explain calmly to the teacher that you did not do it.

- Keep quiet and say nothing.

- Tell the teacher who it was.

- Wait until the end of the class and then explain to the teacher that you did not do it.

- Storm out of the class crying.

- Sit quietly and cry.

- Tell a parent after school.

At this stage it is fine to have some really silly suggestions and some that clearly would not be very successful. Talk about each solution and about what might happen if your child tried each of these responses, and work out the advantages and disadvantages of the various alternatives. Then help your child to decide which solution is likely to produce the best results. In some instances your child might decide that a combination of different solutions, rather than just one of the actions, would be best.

One thing we have found helpful is to ask children to watch their classmates carefully to work out how these other young people deal with different situations. For example, you could ask your child to discover successful ways that classmates use to join in group activities. This "investigating" approach can be used to find solutions to many different social challenges.

ROLE-PLAY

Role-play involves creating an imaginary situation in which you and your child act out a scenario. The idea is for your child to practice his or her social skills by attempting to deal with a pretend situation. The aim in role-play is to make things as realistic as possible. Before children can start to practice in real-life situations, it's best for them to practice in the safety of their home, with someone they trust (you).

Here are some examples of situations that you can role-play with your child. In the more complex situations, you may need to problem solve the scenario first. Choose from the following scenarios to role-play with your child:

- *Starting a conversation.* A new student starts in your class. You decide to ask this new child what his or her name is and where he or she comes from. (Parent plays the part of the new student.)

- *Starting a conversation.* The teacher asks you to do an errand with a student who you don't know very well. You have to walk over to the school office together. (Parent plays the part of the other child.)

- *Maintaining a conversation.* You start at a new school and are sitting in the playground. Another student comes over and sits down in the next seat and asks you how you like the school. You have to answer and then ask a question. (Parent plays the part of the other child.)

- *Asking to join in.* The teacher instructs all the children in the class to find a group and help to produce a poster for the school open house. You look around and see that the other kids have already gotten into groups. Problem solve how you might go about joining one of the groups. Role-play how you might approach a group of classmates and ask to join in. (Parent plays the part of another child in a group.)

- *Asking for information.* A parent tells you to go into the local store and buy some tomato sauce. You can't find it and have to ask the store clerk where it is kept. (Parent plays the part of the store clerk).

- *Asking for information.* You don't hear what the teacher says when he or she gives an instruction in class. You have to ask the teacher to repeat the instruction. (Parent plays the part of the teacher.)

- *Offering help.* A classmate drops his or her homework papers all over the ground, and you decide to offer to help to pick them up. (Parent plays the part of the other child.)

- *Giving a compliment.* You want to give a compliment to the student sitting in the next seat in class. The other student has done some really excellent art work. (Parent plays the part of the other child.)

- *Offering an invitation.* You have won a couple of free tickets to go to the movies. Problem solve how you might invite someone from your class to go along to the movies. Then role-play the chosen response. (Parent plays the part of the other child.)

- *Offering an invitation.* You have a birthday party coming up. Brainstorm how you might go about inviting some classmates or other children. Then role-play how to offer the invitation. (Parent plays the part of a classmate.)

- *Offering help.* A classmate has forgotten his or her lunch, and you decide to offer half of your sandwich. (Parent plays the role of the child who has forgotten his or her lunch.)

- *Owning up.* You borrow a ball from a kid on your street and then lose it. Brainstorm possible solutions to this problem and decide upon the best solution. Imagine that you decide to tell the other child about having lost the ball and explain that you have brought a new ball to replace it. Role-play this situation. (Parent plays the part of the other child.)

- *Apologizing.* You drop your parents' favorite plate in the kitchen, and it breaks. You are clearing up the pieces when one of your parents walks in. Brainstorm this situation and work out the best solution. Imagine that you decide to apologize to your parent and role-play this scenario. (Parent plays the part of the parent.)

- *Asking for information.* Your teacher assigns some work in class, and you do not understand what you are supposed to do. Brainstorm different solutions to this problem. You wait behind after class and ask the teacher to explain. (Parent plays the part of the teacher.)

- *Saying no.* Another child is trying to convince you to loan out your favorite possession. You are worried that he or she will break it and know that you should say no. (Parent plays the part of the child trying to borrow the item.)

- *Sticking up for yourself.* A parent yells at you for breaking a window, but you didn't do it. Brainstorm possible solutions to this problem and decide upon the best solution. Imagine that you decide to explain that you did not do it. Role-play this situation. (Parent plays the part of the parent.)

- *Dealing with teasing and bullying.* Specific strategies are discussed later in this chapter in the section, "Dealing with Teasing and Bullying."

GIVING FEEDBACK AND PRAISE

When children are learning new skills, they can only improve if they're given feedback about whether their performance is correct or whether some changes need to be made. When children start to practice their new skills, they may not be very competent at first. It's really important that you look for good things in their performance and give them plenty of praise for trying. They must not feel as if they've failed. You should praise early attempts even if they are doing only a little bit better; expect them to get better and better over time. In particular, you need to focus on the good things about your child's performance and tell your child what he or she did well (e.g., "That was a great try. I really liked the way you smiled when you told me your name"). If you are giving feedback about something that needs improvement, this should be phrased in a gentle and encouraging way. For example, if your child is not making eye contact during a conversation, you could say, "Well done. I really liked the questions you asked. Now try that again and see if you can look at me just a little."

Practicing in the Real World

Once your child is able to use these new social skills at home in practice sessions with you, he or she will need to practice them in real-life situations. It is important that you set some small homework tasks for real-life practice after each session. These tasks need to be simple and relatively easy to perform. There is no point in children trying something far too hard and then failing miserably. They will not be likely to try again in the future, and their worst fears will have come true. You might want to talk to your child's teacher and explain to him or her about the program you are doing. The teacher might have some good ideas about very simple social tasks that your child could try. He or she might even organize some small group situations for your child where practice would be easier.

Some real-life tasks in which to practice specific body language or voice skills could include the following:

- Say good morning to the teacher.

- Say hello to a particular child (preferably pick a sociable, friendly child to begin with).

- Ask a question of a relative when he or she comes to visit.

- Practice asking questions with a brother or sister.

- Ask a particular child what his or her favorite TV show is.

- Ask a particular child whether he or she has any pets.

It is a good idea to organize these practices into a stepladder just like you are doing with your child's feared situations.

Only one task should be set after each home practice session. It is helpful to write the task down on a card. The card should describe what the task is and with whom, where, and when it is to be performed. Then the card should have a space to record when the task was completed and any difficulties encountered. The practice cards can be used with most children over the age of seven, depending on reading and writing abilities. With very young children, you may need to prompt the practice of skills by attending playgroups or activities with them.

It is also a good idea to prepare children for ways of handling situations in the event that they do not work out well. For example, it can be devastating to ask to join in a group for the first time only to be rejected by the group. You need to prepare children to use their detective thinking to handle things if their early attempts are not very successful. It is also important for you to help children set realistic goals that are within their capabilities. Many anxious children will be only too ready to interpret a reasonable attempt as failure. If possible, you might want to ask the help of a teacher who can prompt your child on the first couple of occasions. Teachers may also be able to observe from a distance and increase the chance of a successful outcome by discreetly arranging the situation.

PUTTING SOCIAL SKILLS AND ANXIETY MANAGEMENT SKILLS TOGETHER

Once your child begins to practice these skills in real-life situations, it is important to remember that this part of the social skills program should fit together with the anxiety management methods that your child has learned, including detective thinking and stepladders. In many cases learning to deal with new social situations should become part of your child's stepladder. Your child should not be pushed to tackle a social situation when it is still too difficult for him or her, though. If a particular social skill is still too difficult, remember to break this goal down into smaller, simpler steps. For example, if your child is working on the skill of eye contact, a mini-stepladder might look like this:

Goal: To look a person in the eyes while doing the following tasks

1. Talk to my teacher for thirty seconds; look at her at least three times.

2. Order myself a takeout meal and look at the person when I order.

3. Talk to my neighbor for two minutes and keep good eye contact with her.

4. Ask the gym teacher to open the sports cupboard during recess; look at him while asking.

5. Talk for five minutes to the basketball coach; make eye contact.

In addition, many of the stepladders that you and your child have planned will include social contacts. It is very important to remind your child to use these opportunities to practice his or her social skills.

Creating Social Opportunities

In addition to teaching social skills, parents can help by setting up opportunities for children to practice their social skills. Anxious children often avoid places such as clubs where children have the chance to interact with each other. For example, many anxious children protest at the thought of going to a social or activity club, church groups, study groups, chess clubs, or sports clubs. It is a good idea to make a list of all of the social clubs and activities for young people in your area. Libraries, government services, the phone book, or the Internet might provide some of this information. Together with your child, you can work out which club or activity would be of greatest interest. You may find quite a bit of resistance to the idea from your child. However, it is really worth encouraging your child to attend events where he or she would be with other children. You might be able to help by arranging contacts with another family whose child belongs to a particular group. Remember, if it seems too frightening for your child to do this, then it is a useful thing to do. Create a stepladder with the club or group at the top and break it down into smaller steps.

EXPLAINING SOCIAL SKILLS TO CHILDREN

You have read about ways of developing your child's social skills. Ultimately, the goal is for children to be able to act confidently when they need to; this is the culmination of learning to use good social skills. To explain to children the difference between good and poor social skills, compare assertive behavior with unassertive (too weak) or aggressive (too strong) behaviors. Even if you find that your child is confident in all areas of social skill, awareness of the differences between assertive, passive, and aggressive behaviors, and some practice in using assertiveness when needed, is useful.

In this section, all of the basic social skills are summarized by seven prompting words: "eyes," "posture," "voice," "content," "feelings," "appearance," and "behavior." This makes it easier for children to focus on one aspect of assertiveness at a time until they are ready to put them all together. Remember that these skills progressively build on each other, so if your child is weak in the areas of body language or voice quality, you should focus on these first before working on conversation, friendship, and high-level assertiveness skills such as standing up for yourself. The following table—Passive, Aggressive, and Assertive Actions— summarizes some of the observations that children may make about assertive, passive, and aggressive ways of behaving toward people.

PASSIVE, AGGRESSIVE, AND ASSERTIVE ACTIONS

	Passive (too weak)	Aggressive (too strong)	Assertive (just right)
Eyes	Eyes and head down	Stares	Looks in the eyes but not for too long
Posture	Hunched over, stands back too far	Leans over the top of other people, gets very close to them	Stands straight, confident body language
Voice	Quiet, mumbling voice	Speaks sarcastically, loud voice	Clear, pleasant voice
Content	"I'll forget about it." "I don't really care." "I'm all right." "I don't mind."	"Don't touch me." "You're just as bad." "Shut up, moron." "You don't know what you're talking about."	"I don't like you doing that." "I am angry with you." "I need to get some help."
Feelings	Miserable, bottles it up, hurt	Angry, jealous	Confident, content
Appearance	Doesn't smile often, looks sad	Angry face, rigid, looks tense	Appears calm and in control, neutral look
Behavior	Does nothing, pays back quietly, complains	Blames, provokes, throws or breaks things, attacks, retaliates	Seeks help, stands up for self in a pleasant manner, takes risks, and, when safe, says what he or she thinks, feels, and wants

Just as when they are learning basic social skills, children should practice behaving assertively first in role-play and then in real life. The more practice they have at behaving assertively, and the more praise they get for choosing to interact that way, the more likely it is that your child will be able to interact with others effectively.

DEALING WITH TEASING AND BULLYING

Sadly, anxious children who are quiet, unassertive, and possibly awkward can sometimes become a target for bullies. Luckily, most anxious children are not teased or bullied but, if they are, this can really add to their worries and can lead to poor self-esteem and depression. If you discover that your child is being teased or bullied, acting quickly and calmly to help your child deal with the problem will be very important.

How to React as a Parent

Bullying and teasing are an unfortunate part of the reality of childhood. As a parent, your first instinct when hearing about bullying will probably be to get angry and you will want to step in and see that the bully is appropriately punished. However, this will not necessarily stop your child from being teased in the future, and it probably won't make your child feel better about him- or herself. When you realize your child is being teased or bullied, you need, first of all, to show concern and sympathy for your child—he or she may not want you to do anything (yet), but may just want to talk it through. Do not let *your* hurt, pride, or anger get in the way of helping your child to solve *his* or *her* problem. Make sure you give your child permission to swear and say things that he or she would not normally be allowed to say at home so that he or she can talk about all that is happening. Talking about it will help to take the hurt and shame out of the teasing.

Often, you will need to help your child to work out whether the other child is trying to be friendly and fooling around (even though that child's behavior has been hurtful) or whether the other child is being cruel. If it's the former, then you need to help your child to learn to laugh along or to be honest that the teasing has upset him or her (in other words—to be assertive). If it's deliberate cruelty, then you need to help your child to work out a different way of reacting so that he or she can take control of the bully's game.

It is important to involve school personnel if your child is not able to stop the teasing within a short space of time or if the bullying is in any way physical. Most schools have bullying policies—give the school a chance to implement their policy but ask when you should check back with them, and do so. Be persistent but never accuse any person of being incompetent or uncaring—it will not help your child's situation. Expect the school to take action but do not be surprised if they suggest changes for your child, including how your child interacts with other children. Although teasing and bullying should not take place and the responsibility for stopping it is with the bully, bullies choose easy targets—that is, those children who are not assertive and who get upset or angry when teased. By teaching your child to outsmart the bully, you are providing him or her with constructive strategies for self-protection.

How to Outsmart a Bully

Children can use these four approaches to outsmarting a bully:

1. Children need to talk about the teases until they don't hurt anymore. By making jokes out of the teases, unkind words can lose their power. Your child can also use detective think-ing to establish if the tease is true or not. If it is true, a child can problem solve how to fix the situation. If it is not true, he or she will realize that there's no need to believe the tease— the bully is wrong.

2. Children also need to stay close to a sympathetic audience such as friendly children or teachers. It can take some planning to work out who will be sympathetic or, for example, how to stay close to others when walking home (children might need to change their route slightly). One clever way to get attention is to make the bully make more noise by saying, "Sorry I didn't hear you; can you say that a bit louder?" "I still can't hear you," and so on until the bully has to shout the tease. When the bully shouts, it will probably get him or her in trouble, or it might get other children to step in.

3. Your child's motto needs to become—"Do something different." Bullies tease and push to get the typical reaction of fear, sadness, or anger from their victims. Doing anything that shows the bully that the tease hasn't bothered your child will take all of the fun out of teasing. Brainstorming ways of doing things differently and practicing those differences can be helpful in building your child's confidence. For example, a child might try to ignore the bully, laugh at him- or herself (it is usually not a good idea to laugh at the bully), hum to him- or herself, or point out how pretty the sun is today.

4. Rather than reacting to the tease in an emotional way, children can develop clever comebacks. For example if a bully says, "You're a fat pig," rather than yelling, "I am not, you *!@$," a child could respond, "Gosh, I was aiming for 'enormous elephant' this week; I'll have to keep trying." Such a response is going to confuse the bully enough to make time for the child to move out of the line of fire. It is very important that your child is not nasty, rude, or aggressive to the bully since this might simply make the situation worse. Rather, your child can try to diffuse the situation and show the bully that what was said doesn't hurt (even if at first it does).

5. Using these last two techniques takes practice and planning. Even though you will probably find this very hard to do, one excellent practice is for you to pretend to be the bully and to

yell out nasty things to your child who can then practice a new way of reacting or a new comeback until he or she is able to do this easily. Once your child can do these things without thinking, he or she can use them in real life.

IMPORTANT: If your child is having serious problems with teasing and bullying, you should consider seeking professional help on this issue.

ACTIVITIES TO DO WITH YOUR CHILD ...

CHILDREN'S ACTIVITY 25: WHY BE A CONFIDENT PERSON?

Talk to your child about why it is useful to be a confident person and about different ways of communicating. Have a look at the Passive, Aggressive, and Assertive Actions table earlier in this chapter and make a copy on a sheet of paper with the same rows and columns, but nothing written in the boxes. (There is also a blank copy in the workbook on the Internet at www.ceh.mq.edu.au/hyac .html.) Help your child to complete the table by writing in some of the ways they typically act when they need to act assertively and then go back and help them to write down some better ways of acting. If your child has trouble coming up with examples of these behaviors, try to get him or her to think of some times recently when they have been asked to do something they didn't want, or wanted to ask a difficult favor of someone, and so on.

CHILDREN'S ACTIVITY 26: USING ASSERTIVE BEHAVIOR

You will already have an idea of what social skills your child needs to improve. Use a variety of situations to coach your child on using these particular skills and ultimately on being assertive. Role-play situations such as someone pushing in front of you in a line, a neighbor borrowing a bike without asking, asking someone where a product is in the supermarket, and seeing an older child picking on a younger child in the playground. You can also use the list of situations in the "Role-Play" section for further practice. As a first step, discuss the situation so that you and your child can come up with an ideal picture of that situation (that is, the way it would happen if someone was being assertive). Once this is worked out, role-play the solution. Make this fun—if your child has trouble seeing the right way to be assertive, have him or her role-play the worst possible solution (e.g., being passive) and then role-play the alternate (assertive) solution. Swap roles occasionally so that you can model good use of the skills. If the early social skills (like eye contact or voice volume) need work, try to role-play a couple of situations each day.

CHILDREN'S ACTIVITY 27: OUTSMARTING BULLIES

Talk with your child about the different ways to outsmart a bully, including talking about it to someone you trust, getting an audience who may help if needed, doing something differently than you would normally, and developing clever comebacks that you can say to diffuse a situation. You will need to give your child examples of comebacks such as, "Tease: You're a jerk. Comeback: Only on Tuesdays." "Tease: You're fat. Comeback: Don't be ridiculous—I'm enormous." "Tease: Four-eyes. Comeback: *Wish* I had four eyes; then I wouldn't need these glasses."

When giving examples of comebacks, have your child say a tease and then you give a comeback. Hopefully your child will laugh. Ask your child to think of some things that have been said to him or her (or to friends) as teases. Then work together to come up with appropriate comebacks that could be used as responses if that is said to your child again. Your child will need to practice using these comebacks in different situations before trying it with a bully. You could even practice a tease a day: you pop up every so often with the tease, and your child responds with the comeback. You could pop the tease in while eating dinner, traveling in the car, or watching TV. At first say it in a lighthearted manner, slowly increasing the severity of your tone as your child gains confidence with responding to each tease. Once he or she sounds confident and can say it instantly, have your child practice at school.

If your child is being bullied or teased, help him or her to apply the out-smarting-bullies tactics to the unique situation, give your child the opportunity to practice reacting differently at home, and then have him or her try at school. Before your child tries the new approach, it can be helpful to discuss what to do if the bully doesn't back off. A good attitude is that if at first you don't succeed, try again—with small changes to the plan. *However, it is important to remember that if the teasing doesn't stop, or if it escalates into physical bullying, the school and professional help need to be involved.*

CHILDREN'S PRACTICE TASK 7: ASSERTIVE BEHAVIOR AND CONTINUED PRACTICE

In addition to continuing to work on stepladders (for which you should discuss and plan steps for the week ahead) and practicing other anxiety management skills as opportunities arise, your child should make an effort to practice assertive behavior, either in role-play or real life. It can be helpful to create a checklist that reminds your child of what assertiveness looks and sounds like to encourage him or her to concentrate on the behaviors that he or she most needs to improve in terms of social skills.

CHAPTER HIGHLIGHTS

In this chapter, you and your child learned ...

- Social skills are important, and children need to develop certain types of social skills to be successful.

- Social skills build on each other, and children need to know basic skills such as eye contact before they can successfully learn more difficult skills such as starting a conversation or giving a compliment.

- There are different ways of teaching social skills, such as discussing appropriate skills, and using modeling and role-play. The latter can be a good way to teach children who have more extensive difficulties.

- There are differences between passive, aggressive, and assertive behavior.

- A person looks and behaves a certain way when being assertive.

- There are different ways of outsmarting bullies, including talking to reduce the hurt, staying close to friendly children and adults, planning ways to react differently when teased or bullied, and learning some clever comebacks to use in response to a tease.

Your child will need to do the following:

- Complete the children's activities with the help of a parent or other adult.

- Practice behaving assertively in everyday situations or, for children who struggle more extensively with social skills, practice one new social skill at a time using role-plays at home and then in the real world.

- Continue to work on stepladders and continue to practice other anxiety management skills such as realistic thinking and problem solving. (Your child should be quite a way up a few of his or her stepladders by now.)

CHAPTER 9

Taking Stock

BRINGING IT ALL TOGETHER

In previous chapters, we took you through a number of techniques or strategies to help your child manage his or her anxiety. In this chapter we will briefly summarize what we have covered and then we will discuss how the various strategies fit together and how they can be combined into a comprehensive program to help your child. We will illustrate this by looking at the specific programs that we planned for the five children who we introduced at the beginning of this book.

What We Have Covered So Far

In chapters 1 and 2 we discussed what anxiety is and how you can recognize anxiety and fear in your child. We also discussed ways in which your child can learn to understand more about his or her feelings. We supplied exercises to help you teach your child about the three features of anxiety: physical feelings, mental activity, and behaviors. We also introduced the idea of recording your child's anxiety using our ten-point worry scale. By this stage, your child should be getting pretty good at rating his or her degree of anxiety and should realize that anxiety varies from situation to situation.

We also explained to you a little of where anxiety might come from, and hopefully this gave you some understanding of why your child might be anxious. In chapter 1, we described some of the things that keep your child anxious in the here and now and we explained the various techniques we would cover. These techniques included realistic thinking, stepladders, and building of social skills.

Realistic thinking helps your child change his or her current ways of thinking about frightening situations (as discussed in chapter 3). We suggested that anxious children (and adults) tend to think unrealistically and regularly look at the negative in situations. In particular, anxious children overestimate *how likely* it is that bad things will happen and they catastrophize about *how bad* those things will be. We provided an exercise to help your child realize that his or her feelings could be changed if he or she could learn to think differently about situations. Most importantly, we offered a way that your child could learn to think like a detective and look for evidence regarding his or her beliefs. The following points were made:

- Your thoughts and beliefs directly cause your feelings in a situation.

- Worried thoughts cause you to feel more anxious. Calm thoughts cause you to feel more relaxed.

- You need to act like a detective in frightening situations and look for evidence for your worried thoughts.

- There are many types of evidence you can look for. Some of the best sources of evidence come from previous experience and alternative explanations.

- Using the evidence, a calm thought can be found that you can use in the anxious situation.

In chapter 6, we discussed how to simplify detective thinking by using questions and thoughts that work well for your child.

Using stepladders is the crucial technique to encourage your child to face up to his or her fears and these were introduced in chapter 5. Stepladders are most likely to work when they are implemented in a consistent and systematic way. There are several steps to creating stepladders:

- Brainstorm all of the situations your child fears and avoids.

- Group them together into similar or related fears.

- Organize the fears so that your child has a series of stepladders, each made of small steps.

- Have your child begin with the first step of each stepladder and gradually work his or her way up to the top.

- Reward each successful attempt at a step. Unsuccessful attempts should be rewarded in a smaller way to acknowledge the effort that was put in.

There are also several ways to increase the chance that stepladders will work:

- Make sure the steps are not too far apart.

- Repeat each step several times until your child is more or less bored with it.

- Give rewards when promised, and as soon as possible after a step is completed, to keep your child's motivation going.

- Make sure that the stepladder includes the outcomes that your child is really afraid of.

There are a number of ways that the effects of stepladders can be maximized, but keep in mind that developing stepladders for some of the more subtle or complex forms of anxiety can be difficult. We discussed ways of producing more creative stepladders and fixing problems with stepladders in chapters 6 and 7.

In chapter 8 we discussed your child's social skills, that is, the way your child interacts with other people. Many anxious children have no problems with social skills, and if this is true for your child, this component can be left out of his or her program. But if your child does lack some social skills, it's important to address this in order to give him or her as many positive experiences as possible. We described a number of exercises you could use with your child to help him or her understand more about how to develop various social skills. When teaching your child social skills, we suggested the following strategies:

■ Teach one skill at a time.

■ Make the lessons fun and keep them short.

■ Give your child feedback about his or her current ways of acting and then show him or her better ways to act.

■ Provide opportunities for your child to get lots of practice.

■ Begin with the more basic skills and gradually build to more difficult ones.

We also suggested that practicing assertive behaviors, such as standing up for yourself and dealing with teasing, will help to build all children's confidence.

Finally, don't forget chapter 4 on parenting skills where we discussed both the ways in which you might accidentally increase your child's anxiety and the ways you could better handle it. Some of the main points we made were as follows:

■ Protecting or taking over for your child may make him or her feel better in the short run but will maintain his or her anxiety over time. It is more useful to encourage your child to face his or her fears.

■ If your child asks for help, it is best to give guidance in how to solve the problem and then encourage your child to solve it for him- or herself.

■ If your child regularly asks for reassurance, you should again give guidance in how to solve the problem (e.g., realistic thinking) and then let your child know that you will ignore further requests for help.

- Remember to reward your child for behaviors that you are happy with.

- If you find it difficult to let your child make his or her own mistakes, you need to do realistic thinking yourself to convince yourself that your child will not suffer in the long run if things do not always go well.

Some Sample Programs

It is not always necessary to use every one of these techniques and components with each child. Some types of problems need certain techniques more than others, and some children will find that some techniques make more sense to them than others do. Therefore, even though it is important for you and your child to understand all of these techniques, you may find that the program you and your child choose does not necessarily use each of the techniques we have covered. We will now revisit the five children we've mentioned throughout this book and describe the final program each of them selected. You will notice that the most essential technique—stepladders—was included in each child's program. *Your child will not learn to master his or her fears if he or she does not do lots of stepladder practice.*

TALIA

You may remember that Talia had a fear of water. Overall, she was a confident, outgoing nine-year-old, but Talia was afraid of swimming, and this was starting to affect her confidence with friends.

In this type of case, where the problem is very restricted and the child is not generally shy or sensitive, the program can be a very quick and straightforward one that involves only stepladders. Talia's program, therefore, began with Talia and her parents brainstorming all the sorts of situations that made Talia afraid. They then organized these situations into a stepladder—from easiest to hardest. Because

Talia's fear was a very specific one, it was quite easy to come up with a lot of steps that very gradually got harder and harder. Also, because Talia really wanted to get over her problem and go swimming with her friends, her parents only had to use a few small rewards from time to time to get her to do her practice. Most of the time, they just needed to remind her of her final goal—going to the beach with her friends. The whole program took Talia only about three weeks, and, before long, her fear of water was far behind her.

GEORGE

George had a much broader and more general problem than Talia. He was shy and sensitive and had little self-confidence. Because of his fears, George avoided many social interactions and had few friends. He also had times of feeling low.

Because George's fears were very much a result of the way he thought about things and because he was an intelligent young man, George's parents decided to focus heavily on the realistic thinking component of the program. They spent a great deal of time working on getting George to think more realistically about his abilities and, most importantly, about what other people thought of him. The most important lessons that George needed to learn were these: you can do things well and even if you do something badly, other people will not necessarily think badly of you, and even if they do, it is not the end of the world. George did well with his lessons—but it was hard for him to really believe in those concepts. He did begin to shift his beliefs, but they did not change completely.

To try to really reinforce these new beliefs, George's parents included stepladders in his program. Because George was so unconfident and also a little depressed, he really needed lots of encouragement and motivation to work on what were some pretty difficult tasks. So George's parents made sure that the stepladders had lots of very small steps, and they gave him lots of rewards and encouragement along the way. This meant that George's program took quite a long time—in fact, it became a way of life that George and his parents continued, to some extent, for more than a year. By making sure that the steps were small enough that he managed to do them on most occasions, George was able to have plenty of successes and lots of rewards and encouragement from his parents, which, slowly but surely, began to boost his confidence.

Finally, while doing his stepladders, it became clear to George's parents that he really did lack a few basic skills and the ability to really get along with other kids. This was very understandable given that George had had hardly any friends over the years. In his first year of middle school, George was also starting to be teased by a few of the kids. So George's parents made sure that they also included some work on his social skills in his program. George and his parents practiced different ways of meeting new kids and of talking to them. George then made sure that he practiced these new skills during his stepladders and in daily life. Because the teasing was not too severe, he didn't want his parents to talk to the school teachers about it. Instead, he practiced ways of dealing with the teasing, especially trying to let the other kids know that he was okay with their comments and that they didn't bother him. Luckily, this seemed to be enough, and the teasing stopped after a short while. This success was a huge boost for George's confidence.

George is still working on his anxiety, and it will be a long-term task for him. But over the course of several months, he was already a different boy than the one who began the program. As George's confidence began to build, his depression also became less of an issue. George and his parents were happy with the changes and didn't feel that he needed to do any special work on his earlier low moods.

JESS

Jess had two quite separate problems—constant worry and a fear of choking. At the beginning of the program, the focus was on controlling worry and helping Jess's parents deal with Jess's challenging behavior. Once Jess began working with stepladders, she would be able to begin addressing her fear of choking.

To deal with her worries, Jess focused on learning and then practicing detective thinking. This was very important for her as she constantly expected the worst in all situations. Without having the realistic thoughts in place, Jess would never have agreed to try and face her fears. Jess and her parents got into the habit of looking for evidence for all of the worried thoughts that any of them had as a way of practicing realistic thinking as often as possible. As Jess's skill increased, her parents took less of a role in guiding her through the process until they were able to just say, "What would a detective say about that?"

Jess did two main stepladders that addressed her worries. The first was for increasing her contact with other children, and the second was for getting her work done within a time limit and without trying to make her answers perfect. Jess proceeded slowly with these stepladders. She had a setback on the first stepladder when one of her good friends got annoyed because Jess didn't invite her to her house one weekend. Jess wanted to stop the stepladder there, but after doing a lot of detective thinking work and also looking back at what Jess thought life would be like if she didn't worry so much, she was able to keep working. To increase her confidence, she went back two steps, repeated them, and then kept going.

Jess's fear of choking was addressed with a very long stepladder that involved making a list of all the foods she was scared of eating and then slowly working through the list. For the tough foods, like lamb chops, the steps also involved how small she was able to cut the pieces up and how long she could chew each mouthful. The early steps were quite difficult, but once Jess reached the step of eating a steak sandwich, all the rest of the foods on the lists were easy, and her eating went back to normal very quickly.

Jess had had a long time to practice being fearful and worried, so it took a few months for any noticeable progress to be made. This was frustrating for her parents, but they persisted with implementing the skills, expecting Jess to be able to manage her anxiety. Over time there were breakthroughs, some of which came quickly while others were hard fought. The important thing was that Jess started to gain weight, she could now complete tests at school, and she could get to sleep without needing to worry about things that might happen the next day.

KURT

Kurt had two main problems—repetitive washing because of a fear of germs and a more generalized anxiety that affected all sorts of different areas. Because of the complexity of these problems, Kurt's first step was to be very clear about all of the behaviors and features that went with each type of difficulty. Kurt labeled his anxieties his "washing problem" and his "worry problem" so that he could keep them straight in his head. There were a lot of similarities between the two problems, but there were also some differences that Kurt needed to be clear on.

Kurt's father was not interested in helping, but Kurt and his mother worked on the program together. They began by working on realistic thinking. For his washing problem, Kurt needed to learn that he was not picking up lots of germs and that even if he was, they would not hurt him. For his worry problem, Kurt needed to learn the general rule that the world was not a particularly dangerous place and that he was not especially likely to get hurt. Because there were so many things that Kurt worried about, it was quite easy to think of lots of evidence to prove to himself that he was not thinking realistically. Kurt was able to begin to use his detective, James Bond, to help him through some tough situations.

As with all the other programs, Kurt's included stepladders. Kurt's stepladders were a little harder to think up because his worries were so much less concrete than the other children's. But by thinking hard, Kurt and his mother were able to come up with several stepladders and lots of steps. In chapter 6, we gave you some examples of creative stepladders for Kurt and other children who had these less concrete fears. The especially hard part for Kurt came when he had to go through several days without washing. But his determination and the rewards his mother used helped him get through it. After many weeks, it began to get easier.

LASHI

Lashi was a young girl whose parents had separated. She worried that her mother might be injured or killed and that she would never see her again. As a result, she became upset whenever she had to separate from her mother. Because Lashi was only seven, her mother decided to use calm thoughts on cue cards instead of full realistic thinking and she also taught Lashi relaxation skills. The relaxation fit with her mother's general philosophy in life since she, herself, had done several relaxation courses over the years.

Lashi really enjoyed the relaxation, especially because it gave her some special time alone with her mother. She never really learned to completely relax, but she was able to do it enough that it gave her the start that she needed before moving on to stepladders.

The stepladders were the main part of Lashi's program. Lashi and her mother worked out a number of stepladders for different portions of her problem—going to school, staying overnight at other people's houses, being left with a sitter, and so on. Each stepladder was broken down into small steps, and Lashi picked some fun rewards for doing each one. Many of the rewards involved special time with her mother. Part of the program also involved Lashi's mother not allowing Lashi to ask for too much reassurance.

Lashi's mother also realized that the separation had affected *her* in many ways too. Most importantly, she realized that following the breakup of the relationship, she became more scared of losing Lashi. As a result, she had started to be a little too protective of Lashi and was perhaps a bit too forgiving of her fears. Lashi's mother had to admit that sometimes when she let Lashi stay home from school, she really didn't mind too much. So Lashi's mother decided to work on being a little less protective herself and to be tougher in encouraging Lashi to face her fears. As part of this change, Lashi's mother began to do some realistic thinking about her own worries—what would really happen if Lashi became a little scared, would Lashi really hate her if she made her go to school, and so on.

Finally, when Lashi was doing pretty well in separating from her mother, she and her mother worked out another stepladder for Lashi's other fears of injections and hospitals. Because both of Lashi's areas of fear—separating from her mother and injections—were quite concrete, the program for Lashi was fairly straightforward and it was not long before she started to show some great improvements. The whole program was done in around twelve weeks.

ACTIVITIES TO DO WITH YOUR CHILD ...

CHILDREN'S ACTIVITY 28: HOW COULD I HELP OTHERS

As a way of consolidating your child's anxiety management skills, it can help to have your child "help" other children who have similar problems. By helping others, children are consolidating their own skills and also preempting fears and worries that they may one day face. This is a useful preventative task and also boosts self-confidence as children realize that they have useful knowledge.

Make up several stories of other children who have anxiety and ask your child to come up with ideas for how those children could learn to cope better. Discuss each "case" with your child and have him or her suggest what each child might do to overcome anxiety. Cases might include the following:

- Jack has a fear of bugs; he feels sick when he sees them and has to leave any situation where he sees a bug even if it is only on TV.

- Annie has her first summer camp coming up; she has never stayed away from home and is worried about what might go wrong.

- Melissa started a new school last year; she hasn't made very many friends and has become really shy.

- Tim worries all the time about his mum getting sick or hurt. He tries his best to always bo with her so that he can take care of her.

- Sam is starting high school next year and is really nervous. He worries about getting lost in the large school, finding the work difficult, making friends, and what the teachers will be like. His worries make it difficult to get to sleep.

CHILDREN'S PRACTICE TASK 8: REACHING MY GOALS

The final practice task asks children to put in extra effort in reaching the goals on their stepladders. They should plan when they will face steps and what coping skills they can use to help them manage their anxiety. You will need to keep repeating this practice task for several weeks or possibly several months, depending on the complexity, number, and length of your child's stepladders. Each week, help your child to make appropriate plans and help him or her implement chosen steps.

CHAPTER HIGHLIGHTS

In this chapter, you and your child reviewed ...

- An overview of all the skills taught in this program

- A summary of how the children featured in this book completed their individual programs

- The challenge of working out how to help other children who are experiencing fears and worries

Your child will need to do the following:

- Complete the children's activity with the help of a parent or other adult.

- Continue to work on stepladders, hopefully nearing the top.

- Continue to practice other anxiety management skills such as realistic thinking, problem solving, and behaving assertively.

CHAPTER 10

Planning for the Future

HOW FAR HAVE WE COME?

Congratulations—you are coming to the end of the program. If you and your child have worked through the chapters and exercises in this book carefully, it has probably been a long, hard road. Hopefully, it has also been a worthwhile one. Your son or daughter should be quite a different child from the one who started the program. Of course, change can range from large to small—everyone is different, and how much your child has changed will depend on so many things.

MAINTAINING GAINS

Probably the main question on your mind now is, where do we go from here? How long do we keep practicing, and when can we put all this behind us and forget all about it? Unfortunately, these questions don't have clear-cut answers. Every child is different, and every situation varies. Some children we have treated make huge gains in a few short weeks and never look back. Others change slowly and to only a small degree and may really need to keep their practice going for months or even years. The typical child is probably somewhere in between. He or she may practice hard for ten to fifteen weeks and make positive changes. At this point, these children can stop doing the set, formal practices, but they and their parents need to keep in mind all that they have learned, and continue to do so for the rest of their lives. They need to keep reminding themselves of the principles of realistic thinking and stepladders and, whenever they get a chance, they should do the occasional practice. This doesn't mean having to do formal practice, but simply, that they should practice whenever life throws something a little tough their way. For example, when your child has exams or a big sporting event or perhaps has to give a speech at an awards night, it's a chance for your child to remind him- or herself of the techniques learned here. If your child finds that his or her anxiety is high, it is a chance to practice the techniques properly again for a week or so, just to get back on top of things. The practice your child has to do should not be too painful over time because many of the techniques should become a natural and normal part of his or her life. As your child builds confidence, makes new friends, and has successes, the techniques, such as realistic thinking and social skills and even stepladders, will be something that he or she does anyway as part of living.

Relapse

There is the possibility of what professionals call *relapse*, that is, that at some point, your child will once again begin to experience problems with fears and anxiety. This is not necessarily going to happen, and for many children, it never does. But as described in chapter 1, for a variety of reasons, including his or her genes, your child is likely to be a sensitive child, and so there is always the possibility that anxiety will once again rear its head. This may happen for a number of reasons. First, once life starts to feel good again, it is understandable that children and their parents often stop practicing their techniques. Sometimes, in these cases, anxiety just has a habit of very gradually creeping back. Second, bad things do happen in life. Your child may lose someone close to him or her, or he or she could fail an important exam, move to a new house, or be in a car accident. And when something bad happens in life, it makes many of us begin to think for a while that other dangers are very likely. For sensitive children, this might be enough to bring back the negative thoughts and feelings of anxiety. And finally, anxiety and fears can return, in some cases, during times of general stress. For example, if you or your partner become unemployed or if you have a burglary or you separate, these general stresses that enter the family life and affect all of you may cause your child to lose confidence and begin to have fears again.

If relapse does happen, it is not something to panic over. Simply going back to basics and practicing the techniques that worked the first time should get things under control quickly. When your child's return of fear has been triggered by another problem, such as stress within the family or a major calamity, it is important to allow all of you time to deal with that stress first. For example, let's imagine that your partner lands in the hospital after a serious work accident and the whole family is distressed. Your child might lose some confidence, and you may find that some of the fears that he or she had before, or even some new ones, might develop. It is important not to immediately start to do realistic thinking, stepladders, and so on, in a frantic fashion. Rather, allow everyone time to adjust to the changes in your life and to deal with the practical problems and the emotions of the situation first. Once you are starting to get a little control over the stress in your life, then you can begin to practice the anxiety control techniques again.

An important point to remember is that if your child does show some signs of anxiety again, it will take much less time to get on top of that anxiety the second time around. Your child should now know the techniques well and will be able to put them straight into practice. In addition, the anxiety will not have had long to take hold.

We certainly hope that nothing terrible does happen in your child's life and that he or she manages to live a life free of interference from anxiety. But even if there are difficulties along the road, it is good to know that your child has now learned some techniques and skills that will be of benefit throughout the rest of his or her life.

PLANNING FOR THE FUTURE

You have reached the end of the program on learning to manage your child's anxiety. You have also taught your child valuable skills that will no doubt assist him or her in the future when he or she is struggling with other issues. It might be nice to have a family dinner party with all your child's favorite foods as a surprise reward for these achievements.

Taking Time to Chill: Positive and Negative Coping Strategies for Stress

In the future it will be very important to encourage your child to take positive steps to manage general everyday stress. Because your child is probably a sensitive person, learning these skills will help him or her to develop ways of looking after him- or herself in life. Taking a proactive approach to stress will reduce the likelihood of more serious problems, such as continuing anxiety, depression, and substance use. To help your child manage everyday stress, you might, for example, encourage him or her to take up yoga or to practice relaxation, if these are things that he or she would personally find helpful. Ensure that your child devotes time to regular exercise and proper nutrition. It is also especially important for most people to spend time socializing with friends and family. Anxious children have a tendency to focus excessively on tasks such as studying or work. The problem with spending all of their time on any one activity is that they are likely to burn out and they will find it more difficult to achieve their goals. As a parent you need to recognize that a balanced life between work (or school), self-care (like exercising), and a social life is crucial to emotional and physical health.

As your child enters adolescence, it will also be important to acknowledge the temptations of negative coping strategies as a way of dealing with stress. It's important to acknowledge that some people cope with stress by using drugs and alcohol, withdrawing from friends and family, and neglecting activities such as diet, sleep, and exercise.

If you discuss these approaches, their disadvantages, and alternative options in an open way with your child, he or she will be more likely to make positive choices in the future.

Planning for Future Challenges

Before finishing the program, it is important to plan for the future. Managing anxiety will take continuing work, as we discussed above. By looking at future events that may cause anxiety and planning for them using the anxiety management skills, you can prevent major setbacks. That is not to say that there will be no times of high anxiety for your child, but with work, the level of anxiety will be no different than what most children experience during their lifetimes. For some children, immediate future plans will include finishing their current stepladders. You and your child will need to review how far you've gotten and how you intend to finish off the steps or goals that are left. For those children who have reached their original goals, it is useful to ask what the next big life challenge will be and set this as a goal that will be tackled with the help of anxiety management skills. For example, if your child is currently in second grade and you know that camp and other group activities you'll want your child to participate in will start in the next few years, you might like to make a long-term goal of preparing for this event by breaking the potential fear down into manageable steps that can be completed well before the event even occurs. Keeping an eye on your child's future skill needs, as well as on current ones, helps you to be proactive in ensuring your child's successes.

PARENT ACTIVITY: PREPARING TO SET GOALS FOR THE FUTURE

Take some time to think of your child's future.

What skills will your child need in the next few years (e.g., for sleep-overs, camp, staying home alone after school)?

_____

_____

_____

_____

What challenges will your child have to face (e.g., starting high school, moving to a new house, having new siblings)?

_____

_____

_____

_____

Use these ideas to plan long-term goals with your child.

ACTIVITIES TO DO WITH YOUR CHILD ...

CHILDREN'S ACTIVITY 29: WHAT HAVE YOU ACHIEVED?

Talk with your child about how far he or she has come over the past few months, and don't allow a discounting of these achievements. Your child has learned new skills that have enabled him or her to face the things he or she used to worry about, and that is a very big accomplishment. Tell your child what you are proud of about these recent achievements—and give special praise for the effort put in as well as for the fears that he or she has conquered.

Also have your child acknowledge any goals that he or she is still working toward and then you can both talk about when and how to tackle these. It can help to write down new goals that your child can keep working on over the next few months or even a year.

CHILDREN'S ACTIVITY 30: STOPPING FEARS AND WORRIES FROM COMING BACK

Explain to your child that the only way to keep fears and worries under control is to keep practicing your skills (like detective thinking and assertiveness) and to every so often remind yourself that you are strong enough to fight the bad feelings. Your child can do this by facing the once-feared event every now and then as a reminder of how brave he or she now is.

Talk with your child about the possibility that one day he or she might once again feel very scared or worried. Make an agreement that if that's the case in the future, your child will come to you and talk about what is happening, and, in turn, you will give him or her your attention and try your best to understand and give the help he or she needs to face the new challenge. Explain that although your child may feel very anxious at the time, facing fears the second time is usually much quicker and a lot easier than what he or she has been doing over the last few months.

CHILDREN'S ACTIVITY 31: FACING A REALLY BIG CHALLENGE

In this final activity you should ask your child to set a challenge by doing something enjoyable that he or she previously would have avoided or by identifying a big challenge to be faced in the near future (such as going away to camp, starting high school, or joining a sports team). Once an activity is chosen, write an action plan that will help your child to be successful. This might include what needs to be done to start the activity, ways of reducing any anxiety felt, and where your child might be able to get help to achieve the goal. We hope that by aiming to do something challenging that is also enjoyable, your child will also increase social contact, allowing him or her to experience and overcome more anxiety—and ultimately helping your child to perfect his or her anxiety management skills.

CHAPTER HIGHLIGHTS

In this chapter you and your child learned ...

- The progress you have made toward the goals set in the first weeks of the program should be evident.

- It is important to practice anxiety management skills occasionally to ensure that the gains made are maintained.

- Relapses can happen, particularly at times of stress, and when they do, working through the program skills and steps again can quickly overcome the problem.

- It is important to actively manage everyday stress by taking good care of yourself; getting plenty of rest; balancing work, school, and social activities at all times; and avoiding negative coping strategies such as neglecting yourself or your friendships, or using drugs or alcohol.

CONGRATULATIONS!!!

Remember that in activity 5, when you made the family commitment to learning to manage anxiety, you agreed to do a special family activity at the end of the program if you all tried your best. You should plan to do this in the next week. Make sure you all keep to your agreement and enjoy your time together. Give a copy of the certificate on the next page to your child in recognition of his or her effort and achievement.

Congratulations

You are now certified in these important skills:

Brave Behavior

Detective Thinking

Facing Fears

Assertiveness

You should be very proud of all the things you have achieved.

Take a look back at the family commitment. Remember that you agreed that if you all worked very hard at beating fears and worries, you would do a special activity. Now is the time to go and enjoy yourself—you deserve it!

Appendix

RELAXATION

All children experience physical tension in response to stressful events at some time in their lives. Stomachaches, headaches, sleep difficulties, and muscle pains can be related to very high levels of physical tension. Feelings like these can make it difficult for children to use appropriate coping skills, such as detective thinking, as children are too tense to concentrate on using the skills. If your child experiences a high level of physical tension, it may be helpful to teach him or her how to reduce these physical feelings to a level that allows use of the coping skills.

One strategy that children can use to reduce physical tension is relaxation. During relaxation, our body's reactions change so that our heartbeat slows down and our muscle tension decreases. Signs of muscle tightness, such as headaches, gradually disappear. An added advantage is that our thoughts become calm and peaceful, blocking out anxious and worrying issues. These reductions in body tension and worrisome thoughts produce an emotional feeling of calmness and well-being. It's difficult to feel really anxious at the same time that you feel really relaxed. Relaxation might be especially useful for those children who simply can't do the detective thinking.

Some of the different ways that children can learn to relax include listening to soothing, peaceful music; meditation; relaxing imagery;

muscle relaxation exercises; deep-breathing exercises; yoga; and massage. We are going to describe one particular method of relaxation that many children and their parents find effective. One of the best ways to teach children how to relax is to have the whole family involved in practicing and using the relaxation exercises. The method that is presented here combines a variety of techniques, and you may want to adapt the exercises to suit you and your family.

TEACHING YOUR CHILD TO RELAX

Before you start to teach your child how to relax, there are a few points that we need to discuss and that will help you in these teaching sessions.

Relaxation Is a Skill

Like all new skills, relaxation exercises have to be practiced regularly in order to be performed well. You and your child will need to practice every day. To encourage you to practice regularly, we ask you to keep a record of your practice sessions. It is important to fill in a relaxation practice record every time you practice (every day). Suitable forms are included in the workbook at www.ceh.mq.edu.au/hyac.html, or you can create your own using the instructions in the Optional Activity 1 (p. 274). It's a good idea to keep the form in a clearly visible place where you are likely to see it each day (such as the refrigerator). This will help remind both you and your child to do the relaxation practice.

Teaching your child to relax also involves starting at the beginning, teaching the simple steps first. Then, when these can be performed well, you can move on to teaching more complex relaxation skills. It will probably take at least a week of daily practice for your child to relax well. After that, it is important to keep up daily practice while you go through the other steps in this appendix. Relaxation will be a useful technique for children to use when they are trying out some of their anxiety management skills later on.

PICK THE RIGHT TIME

There are several things that you can do to make learning to relax an enjoyable activity. It is important to pick the right time to practice. We suggest that you pick a time when there are no other important things to do. For example, don't pick a time when your child's favorite TV show is on. Many families decide to get up ten to fifteen minutes earlier each day to do their relaxation practice. Others may set aside time before their child goes to bed. Before bed is often a convenient time, but you need to make sure that your child isn't too tired and therefore unable to concentrate on learning the skills. Using relaxation as a way to get to sleep is fine, but practicing relaxation needs to be done at a time when your child can concentrate.

MAKING THE TIME

It is easy to allow relaxation practice to be pushed out by other activities such as homework, sports, TV, and just general living. Setting aside a regular time for relaxation benefits the whole family. It makes everyone in the family aware that life can easily be taken over by the kind of rushing around that makes us forget to look after our emotional well-being.

CREATING A HABIT

One of the best ways of making sure that relaxation practice takes place is to set up a daily habit. Gradually, relaxation will become an automatic activity that is built into the family routine—a daily habit in the same way that brushing our teeth is an automatic task. Try not to start missing days, and have a stand-by time that can be used if your regular practice time is not possible.

CREATING A RELAXING ENVIRONMENT

When your child is learning to relax, you need to create an environment that will encourage relaxation. The area needs to be quiet and one where you will not be disturbed. You may want to take the phone off the hook or put the answering machine on. If you are thinking of inviting visitors over, make sure that it won't conflict with relaxation practice. The place of practice needs to be warm and comfortable. You can use a bed, a comfortable chair, or a mat on the floor. But if you use a bed, make sure you and your child do not fall asleep. Relaxation practice is easier if you and your child are wearing comfortable, casual clothes. Some families like to put on some quiet, calming music. Children respond well to relaxation music, and it may be useful to set the scene for practice by putting this type of music on in the background.

USE PRAISE AND MAKE IT FUN

As with all the methods in this book, you will need to use plenty of praise to encourage your child to practice and use the skills. Remember to give praise for trying, not just for succeeding in relaxation. As much as possible, try to make relaxation time an enjoyable, fun experience. There are plenty of ways to make relaxation practice interesting. In some of the steps, you will be using imagery where children can imagine themselves in peaceful, relaxing situations. You can use wonderful examples here of situations that children will love, such as magical islands, secret gardens, sailing ships, and so on. These will all help to make the sessions interesting and enjoyable.

KEEP IT SIMPLE AND SHORT

Children tend to lose interest quickly and find it hard to pay attention for long periods. With young children, it is better to practice more often for shorter periods, such as five minutes at a time. You also need to use simple language (as we have done in the sample script below) so that your child can understand the instructions.

Teaching by Example

In "Steps to Relaxation," below, you will find a series of steps for learning relaxation skills. Depending on the age of your child, you will probably need to be the teacher of these skills. Some older children and adolescents find it difficult to accept instructions and guidance from their parents and prefer to read through the book and practice the skills on their own. However, one of the best ways to teach young children how to relax is to show them how to perform each step. This involves actually demonstrating each step by doing it yourself. It is really important that with each step you explain out loud exactly what you are doing and why you are doing it. That way, children gradually learn to say these instructions to themselves quietly and can eventually instruct themselves to use the relaxation methods.

The Final Goal

The goal is for children to be able to use their relaxation skills to relax when they become afraid and when they try to face difficult situations. However, it is important to learn the skills really well at home first. Happily, daily relaxation as a habit for the whole family creates an atmosphere of calmness at home that benefits everybody.

STEPS TO RELAXATION

There are several steps to teaching your child to relax. We have provided some sample scripts below to help you explain the ideas to your child. Of course, you don't have to read these scripts out exactly, and if you want to change the words to better suit your style or use words that your child understands better, that is perfectly all right.

Step 1. Learning to Tense and Relax Muscles

One of the best places to start is to learn the difference between being tense and being relaxed. The instructions for step 1 follow. The words in italic are the instructions you should say aloud to your child. You need to perform the actions you're describing as you give your child these instructions. (The words in square brackets are additional prompts for you and should not be read aloud.)

First take your right arm and push it out in front of you. I want you to feel what it is like when your muscles are really tense and tight. Try to imagine that you have a tennis ball in your hand and you are trying to squeeze it really hard. Now really clench your fist and squeeze as tightly as you can. Count slowly to five while you hold it tight: ... 1 ... 2 ... 3 ... 4 ... 5.... Can you tell me how your hand feels when it is all tensed up? What do your muscles feel like? [Encourage your child to come up with words like "tight," "stiff," "gripping."]

Now try again. Really clench your fist and squeeze as tightly as you can. Count slowly to five while you hold it: ... 1 ... 2 ... 3 ... 4 ... 5. Now let go. Let your hand and fingers go limp and loose. Let them go all floppy so that your hand drops back by your side. Can you describe to me how your hand feels when it is relaxed? [Encourage your child to come up with words such as "droopy," "loose," "floppy," or other words that children would use to describe a relaxed state.]

Good—so you can feel the difference in your muscles when they are tense compared to when they are relaxed. What we are going to do in this exercise is to learn to relax the muscles in our bodies so that we can relax at times when we get all tensed up. There are lots of times when we get tensed up, like when we are frightened, nervous, worried, or angry. Relaxing helps you to feel better in difficult times. Learning to relax is just like learning to ride your bike or to roller skate or anything else. You have to practice and, bit by bit, you will find that it gets easier to do. Now you are going in relax your arms even more deeply.

[While you are giving the following instructions, try to keep your voice very calm and peaceful, speaking rather slowly. When you say words like "relax," "calm," and "deeper," make your voice sound very relaxed.]

Push both your arms out in front of you and keep them still and straight. Now push your arms down into your chair or the floor and try to push your body upward, so that your arms are really tight. Now take a deep breath and hold your arms tight, clenching your fists too, while you count to five: ... 1 ... 2 ... 3 ... 4 ... 5. Now let it go. Breathe out and let your arms relax. Make sure that you keep your eyes closed. Let your arms drop down by your sides until they just hang there, limp and loose like a rag doll. Or you could imagine that you are a jellyfish, just a large lump of floppy jelly. Now concentrate on relaxing the muscles in your arms. Try to feel what the muscles in your arms feel like and let them go limp. Check your right arm first and let it go very floppy. Now move your attention to your left arm and let it become heavy and droopy. Relax. Can you feel any tightness? If you can, then try to let your arms go even floppier. Your arms are really starting to relax now—really relaxed, really relaxed, further and further, deeper and deeper, more and more relaxed. Let both arms relax together now. Relax. [Relax quietly for a minute.] *Relax. Really relax.* [Relax quietly for another minute.]*

Good—now in a moment, I am going to ask you to slowly open your eyes. I will count to ten, and when I get to five, I would like you to open your eyes. Then, when I get to ten, I will ask you to slowly sit up ... 1 ... 2 ... 3 ... 4 ... 5. Now slowly open your eyes ... 6 ... 7 ... 8 ... 9 ... 10. Now slowly sit up and have a stretch. How did that feel? How relaxed did you get?

Tensing and relaxing the arms should be repeated two or three times in the session. You can check to see if your child is relaxing well: when you lift your child's arm up, it should drop back gently when you let go. We suggest that you and your child practice step 1 at least twice before moving on to step 2.

Step 2. Relaxing the Rest of the Body

Once your child is able to relax his or her arms really well, you can move on to tense and relax the rest of the body. Begin by relaxing the arms first, as described above. Then, with the arms relaxed, you can move on to other muscle groups. Remember to use a calm, relaxed, and gentle voice while you are giving the instructions.

Now let's move on to the muscles in your head and face. Try to scrunch up your face so that it looks awful. Tighten your eyes, your lips, even your tongue in your mouth. Now take a deep breath and hold it while I count to five: ... 1 ... 2 ... 3 ... 4 ... 5. Now let it go. Breath out and let your face relax. Make sure that you keep your eyes closed. Now concentrate on relaxing the muscles in your face. Feel what your forehead feels like and let it go all limp. Now move your attention to your eyes and let them become heavy and droopy. Relax your mouth and lips. Try to feel what your lips feel like. Can you feel any tightness? If you can, then try to let them go all floppy. Even your tongue should be relaxed, so try to think about what your tongue feels like and relax it. You can relax your whole face and head now, really relax. Your head might even feel as though it is too heavy for your neck. Further and further, deeper and deeper, more and more relaxed—let the whole of your face relax together. Relax. [Relax for a minute.]

Now we are going to tense and relax the lower part of our bodies. This includes our backs, tummies, and legs. This time I want you to imagine that you are a stiff robot. Pull in the muscles in your tummy. Good—now lift your legs up in the air, keeping them straight, and curl up your toes. Really make them tight, just like that metal robot. Now take a deep breath and hold it while I count to five, and keep your legs and tummy tight: ... 1 ... 2 ... 3 ... 4 ... 5. Now let yourself relax. Breathe out through your mouth. Concentrate on relaxing the muscles in your tummy. There shouldn't be any tightness in your stomach muscles now.

Let the muscles go all floppy. Feel what your back feels like too and let it go all limp.

Now move your attention to your legs, and let them become heavy and droopy. Relax the top part of your legs and gradually move down your legs, relaxing each muscle in turn. Relax your knees, your calves, your ankles, and now your feet and toes. Just try to imagine that any tightness and tension is moving down your body, down and down, down through your legs, and out through your toes. Imagine the tightness is drifting out into the air, leaving your body feeling really relaxed, so relaxed that you almost feel like a rag doll. Imagine that I come over and pick you up and shake you. Your legs and arms are all floppy and they shake when I pick you up. There is no tightness in your neck, so your head just drops forward. Your arms and legs just hang there at your sides. Really relax. Further and further, deeper and deeper, more and more relaxed—let all your muscles relax together. Relax.

[Relax for a minute.] *Relax … relax … relax.*

Good—now in a moment, I am going to ask you to slowly open your eyes. I will count to ten, and when I get to five, I'd like you to open your eyes. Then, when I get to ten, I will ask you to slowly sit up … 1 … 2 … 3 … 4 … 5. Now slowly open your eyes … 6 … 7 … 8 … 9 … 10. How did that feel? How relaxed did you get?

It is important to practice going through the different muscle groups, tensing and relaxing them until your child is very good at relaxing all the parts of the body. This step should be practiced every day for two or three days or until your child is able to relax really well. Each time, start with the arms, then the head and face, move on to the legs, and finish with the torso (tummy, bottom, chest, and back). Immediately after relaxation, you might ask your child to show you which parts of the body felt the most relaxed and which still felt tense. This will help you to identify any parts of the body that your child finds hard to relax, and then you can spend some extra time on relaxing this area in the next practice session. Although you are aiming for your child to feel very relaxed, this relaxation does not need to be "perfect."

OPTIONAL ACTIVITY 1: RELAXATION

Explain to your child what relaxation is and how it can help with reducing body symptoms of anxiety. Guide your child through step 1 above, and then incorporate practice of this activity into every day for approximately one week. You can use the relaxation script we provided above, but also consider making a recording of the relaxation instructions so you don't need to read it out each time. It can be a fun thing to do, especially for a child who can read and so can record the instructions in his or her own voice. You should get your child to keep a record of how relaxed he or she becomes each time. Use the relaxation practice record provided in the workbook or create a table with the headings, "Day of the week," "Where did I practice?" "What parts of the body were still tense?" and "How relaxed did I get?"

Step 3. Relaxing the Whole Body at Once

Once children are able to relax each of their body parts in turn, they can move on to relaxing the whole body at once. Children learn relaxation skills at different speeds and speed can also depend on how often they practice the skills. Some children are ready to move on to step 3 after just a couple of days of practicing step 2. Other children may need to work on step 2 every day for two to three weeks before they are able to relax each part of the body really well. But it is also important not to spend too many days on each step, as your child may become bored. We suggest that you and your child decide together when to move on to the next step. Following are the instructions for step 3:

Now let's try to tighten up your whole body at once. Watch me first. I take a deep breath ... scrunch up my face ... push my shoulders up into my neck ... arms pushing down against the chair, stomach pulled in ... and legs lifted upward.... Even my fists are clenched, and my toes are curled up. I hold this while I count to five and then I let go ... 1 ... 2 ... 3 ... 4 ... 5 and breath out and relax. Now you try. Tense up first. Take a deep breath ... scrunch up your face ... push your shoulders up into your neck ... push your arms down against the chair, tummy pulled in ... and legs lifted upward ... clench your fists, and curl up your toes. Make your body go stiff all over. Imagine that you are a robot. Hold it there while you count to five ... 1 ... 2 ... 3 ... 4 ... 5 and now breathe out. Let yourself go all floppy and limp. Imagine that you are a rag doll that doesn't have any bones or stiffness in its body. Let yourself go absolutely limp and loose all over. Let your breathing become gentle now. Just concentrate on letting your body relax, really relax. Close your eyes and try to concentrate on what we're doing. Try not to let other thoughts wander into your head.

Breathe out and let your arms relax. Concentrate on relaxing the muscles in your arms. Let your arms flop down by your sides until they just hang there, limp and loose like that rag doll or that jellyfish. Try to feel what the muscles in your arms feel like and let them go all limp. Check your right arm first and let it go completely limp. Now think about your other arm and let it become heavy and droopy too. Relax. Can you feel any tightness? If you can, then try to let your arms go even floppier. Your arms are really starting to relax now—really relaxed, really relaxed, further and further, deeper and deeper, more and more relaxed. Let both arms relax together now. Relax.

Now let's move onto the muscles in your head and face. Breathe out and let your face relax. Make sure that you keep your eyes closed. Now concentrate on relaxing the muscles in your face. Feel what your forehead feels like and let it go all limp. Now move your attention to your eyes and let them become heavy and droopy. Relax your mouth and lips. Try to focus on what your lips feel like. Can you feel any tightness? If you can, then try to let them go all floppy. Even your tongue should be relaxed, so try to focus on what your tongue feels like and relax it. You can relax your whole face and head now, really relax, further and further, deeper and deeper, more and more relaxed. Let the whole of your face relax, really relax.

Now move your attention to your legs and let them become heavy and floppy. Relax the top part of your legs and gradually move down your legs, relaxing each muscle in turn. Relax your knees, your calves, your ankles, and now your feet and toes. Just try to imagine that any tightness and tension is moving down your body, down and down, down through your legs, and out through your toes. Imagine the tightness is drifting out into the air, leaving your body and legs feeling really relaxed, so relaxed that you can almost feel like that rag doll. Imagine that I come over and pick you up and gently shake you. Your legs and arms are all floppy and they shake when I pick you up. There is no tightness in your neck, so your head just drops forward. Your arms and legs just hang there at your sides, really relaxed, further and further, deeper and deeper, more and more relaxed.

Now think about the muscles in your tummy. There shouldn't be any tightness in your stomach muscles now. Let the muscles go all floppy. Feel what your back feels like too and let it go all limp. Relax. Now I want you to let your muscles relax a little bit more and a little bit more. Last of all, think about relaxing your chest. Can you feel your chest? Really relax the muscles of your chest as you breathe out, really deeply relaxing.

Go back to the top of your head and work downward, checking each muscle that you come to. Check if it feels at all tense or tight. Then say to yourself, "Relax" and let all the tightness drift away. Really relax now. Starting at the top of your head, relax. Moving down … through your arms and chest and down … past your back and your tummy and down through your legs, muscle by muscle, really relaxing. Relax … relax … relax.

Let all your muscles go limp and loose. Imagine waves of tightness leaving your body through your fingers and toes, drifting out into the air, leaving your arms and legs feeling really relaxed and loose, down now through your legs too, past your knees and calves, through your ankles, and out through your toes. Let all the tightness leave your body now, leaving you really relaxed, further and further, deeper and deeper, more and more relaxed. Imagine that you are that rag doll. All limp and loose and floppy. If anyone picked you up, your arms and legs would hang by your sides. There is no tightness anywhere in your body.

Good—now in a moment, I am going to ask you to slowly open your eyes. I will count to ten, and when I get to five, I would like you to open your eyes. Then, when I get to ten, I'd like you to slowly sit up ... 1 ... 2 ... 3 ... 4 ... 5. Now slowly open your eyes ... 6 ... 7 ... 8 ... 9 ... 10. Now slowly sit up. Try not to put all the tension straight back into your muscles. Try to stay relaxed. Good—how did you feel? How relaxed did you get?

By now you and your child (and family, if everyone is taking part) will be getting good at relaxing quickly and deeply. This step usually needs to be practiced every day for at least two to three days or more. Remember that learning to relax is like learning to ride a bike. The more you practice, the easier it will be.

Step 4. Using Breathing and Imagery to Relax Further

Once your child has mastered relaxation of the whole body, it is time to learn to relax even more deeply. There are several ways to increase the depth of relaxation. One method is to use breathing techniques. The aim is to focus attention on breathing in a relaxed way. Make sure that your child doesn't try to breathe too quickly, deeply, or shallowly, or he or she will feel dizzy. The aim is to produce gentle, even, and relaxed breathing.

Focusing on pleasant images or pictures in the mind is also a useful way to relax even more deeply. Our imagination can help us feel deeply relaxed. Children have very good imaginations and are able to relax beautifully with the help of imagery. When you give instructions for imagery, there are certain things that help. You need to describe scenes in a way that helps your child to conjure up the image. You need to describe exactly what can be seen in the picture—the shapes, colors, and textures—as well as the sounds that can be heard, the smells that are there, and any sensations from touch. These details help to create a vivid image. Remember also to select imagery scenes that will appeal to children and that are relaxing in content. The scenes should not be too lively or exciting. The aim is to pick scenes that are likely to produce feelings of deep relaxation, calmness, safety, and peace. The following is one example of this technique. Begin with whole-body relaxation and breathing techniques. Move on to the imagery once your child is reasonably relaxed.

The session should begin by relaxing all the muscles in the body first as described in step 3.

[After tensing the whole body and then relaxing each muscle group in turn ...] *Concentrate on the feelings of the air moving into your lungs and out again. Try to breathe in through your nose and out through your mouth. Concentrate hard on this until you can feel the air moving in through your nose, into your lungs, and then back out through your mouth. The air might feel cool and light. Feel the air moving across your lips on its way out. Now keep your eyes closed and try to imagine that you are holding a candle just in front of you, a few inches from your face but not close enough for it to feel hot. Imagine that as you breathe out, the air moves across your lips and makes the candle flame flicker. Really concentrate on imagining that this is really happening until you can imagine that the candle is really there and flickering. Good—stay relaxed, and with every breath now, I want you to relax a little bit deeper each time you breathe out. Breathe in ... and out ... in ... and out.*

[Try to time this to even, gentle breathing.]

Each time you breathe out, say to yourself, "Relax ... relax." Imagine that the candle flickers each time you breath out as you relax further and further, deeper and deeper, are more and more relaxed. Let your breathing stay even and gentle, not too fast or deep, really gentle and calm. Relax … relax.

Good—now in a moment, I am going to ask you to slowly open your eyes. I will count to ten, and when I get to five, I would like you to open your eyes. Then, when I get to ten, I will ask you to slowly sit up … 1 … 2 … 3 … 4 … 5. Slowly open your eyes … 6 … 7 … 8 … 9 … 10.

Now slowly sit up. Try not to put all the tension straight back into your muscles. Try to stay relaxed. How did you feel?

Now you are going to use your imagination to relax even more deeply. Close your eyes and try to listen to what I am saying. Try not to let your thoughts drift off onto other things. Imagine now that you are lying on the beach. You have plenty of sunscreen on, and it is a warm sunny day. The beach is very quiet. You have had a swim and you are feeling rather tired, so you lie down on your towel. Your friends are having a quiet time too and nobody disturbs you. You lie in the sun and let your body relax. Really relax. You can feel the warmth of the sand through your towel, and your body begins to feel warm and peaceful. You can see the sky—it's clear and blue with only tiny white fluffy clouds. The sea looks clear and blue and sparkles in the sun. You can see a bird flying way up in the sky. Watch the bird as it floats in the wind. Now concentrate on what you can hear. You can hear the sound of the surf gently rolling against the beach. What else can you hear? What else can you see? Now think about what you can feel with your fingers. You reach out and run your fingers through the sand. It feels warm, and the grains of sand run through your fingers. Just imagine that you lie there relaxing, with your muscles becoming more and more relaxed. There is nothing to disturb you. You feel calm and peaceful, no worries, no problems, just really relaxed and calm, further and further, deeper and deeper, more and more relaxed.

Now I want you to spend just a couple of minutes letting your muscles relax a little bit more and a little bit more. Try to keep that scene of being at the beach in your imagination. Just let the whole of your body relax really deeply … further and further, deeper and deeper… . Relax … relax … relax.

Good—now in a moment. I am going to ask you to slowly open your eyes. I will count to ten, and when I get to five, I would like you to open your eyes. Then, when I get to ten, I will ask you to slowly sit up … 1 … 2 … 3 … 4 … 5. Slowly open your eyes … 6 … 7 … 8 … 9 … 10.

Now slowly sit up. Try not to put all the tension straight back into your muscles. Try to stay relaxed. Good—how did you feel? Were you able to imagine being on the beach? Could you imagine the feelings of the sand and the warm sun? How relaxed did you get?

There are many other imagery scenes that can help children to relax. Each session should begin with tensing of the whole body and then relaxation of each muscle starting from the head and working downward. Instructions are then given to concentrate on relaxed breathing, prior to the introduction of a relaxing imagery scene. Here are some ideas that you might like to use to develop some more imagery scripts with your child:

- Lying by the pool at a friend's place

- Lying on a picnic blanket next to a good friend

- Sitting on the porch at Grandma's

- Watching the sunset

- Floating in space

- Watching the rain through a window

- Watching the snow fall

- Lying in front of a log fire

- Camping in the country

- Walking through the autumn leaves

- Watching the stars

- Walking through a secret garden

- Lying in a warm bed, cuddled up to a sleeping puppy

OPTIONAL ACTIVITY 2: WHOLE-BODY RELAXATION

Read the instructions to your child and decide on an imaginary scene that he or she could use when relaxing. Work on the whole-body instructions described above for a few days, and as your child gains confidence and success in doing this, introduce the breathing and imagery instruction. It would be very useful to tape the instructions so that your child could practice without needing your help. Your child can record the results of this practice on the same form you used in the last optional activity. From this record, you can work out which parts of the body are difficult to relax, allowing you and your child to then practice tensing and relaxing these particular muscles until they find it easy to relax them along with the rest of the body.

Step 5. Practicing in Real-Life Situations: Rapid Relaxation

Once your child is able to relax quickly and effectively, he or she can begin to practice in real-life situations. It may take two or more weeks of relaxation practice before you move on to this step. At first, it will be too difficult to relax in stressful and frightening situations. It is best for your child to start by practicing the relaxation skills in real-life situations at times that he or she is not frightened. Then you can gradually teach your child to use relaxation skills in more anxiety-provoking situations.

The relaxation skills that we use in real-life situations involve very rapid tensing and then quick relaxing in a way that is not obvious to other people. These real-world relaxation skills can be used in all sorts of situations, such as in the car, at home, out shopping, in the classroom at school, and many other places where anxiety-provoking events occur. At first, you need to teach your child to use rapid relaxation at home, and then he or she can begin to apply it in other situations. Rapid relaxation does not use imagery. It focuses on quickly relaxing the muscles and on breathing to provide control over the bodily symptoms of anxiety.

Here are the instructions to give to your child:

Now we need to learn how to relax really quickly in situations when other people are around. Take a really deep breath and tense up the whole body ... and hold it tight while we count to five: ... 1 ... 2 ... 3 ... 4 ...5.... Now breathe out slowly and let all the muscles of the body relax together. That's good.

Now try to stay relaxed. Have a quick check to see whether any parts of your body are tight, and relax those muscles as you breathe out. Try to stay really relaxed. No one knows what you are doing. They don't know that you are using your relaxation skills. But you know that you are in control of your muscles and tension. Think to yourself ... I am in control ... I am able to relax, really relax. I can control my breathing ... in ... and ... out ... in ... and ... out ... I can control my muscles—tense and relax, really relax. No one knows what I am doing. I can relax, really relax.

Now it is time for your child to start to practice this rapid relaxation outside the home. Decide together on some times to practice. A good place to start is when you are out together in the car or sitting down to have a drink together in a restaurant or at a café. Prompt children to use the rapid-relaxation method and praise them for their efforts. Check how well they were able to relax. Once your child is able to relax in situations outside the home, you can start to encourage use of the skill when your child is facing frightening situations. You can give a prompt to your child to use rapid relaxation as a coping skill. Relaxation can be a useful skill when your child is working on steps from his or her stepladders.

OPTIONAL ACTIVITY 3: RAPID RELAXATION

· Describe to your child the idea of rapid relaxation. Using the instructions above, try the procedure at home a few times and then several times in routine situations, such as at a restaurant, driving home from school, and in the shopping center. When you feel your child is able to achieve rapid relaxation, start to prompt your child to use it when he or she is feeling tense or notices that his or her worry rating is rising. Keep a record of the times rapid relaxation is used and with what success, using the same relaxation practice record. Later on you should be able to look at the record and identify which situations your child finds more difficult to relax in. When you identify them, you can target some extra relaxation practices in those situations.

Ronald M. Rapee, Ph.D., is professor in the department of psychology at Macquarie University in Sydney, Australia, and director of its Centre for Emotional Health. He has been involved in an advisory capacity with the Diagnostic and Statistical Manual of Mental Disorders and he is a member of the United-States-government-sponsored Project Liberty, which works to develop anxiety management programs for children affected by disasters. He also served on the scientific advisory committee for the Swiss Etiological Study of Adjustment and Mental Health and the editorial board of several international journals.

Ann Wignall, D. Psych, is senior clinical psychologist and director of child and adolescent mental health for Northern Sydney Health Service. She founded the Child and Adolescent Anxiety Clinic at Royal North Shore Hospital and works clinically with children and families with a broad range of anxiety and behavioral disorders.

Susan H. Spence, Ph.D., is professor of psychology and now pro-vice chancellor at Griffith University in Brisbane, Australia. She is a researcher and clinical psychologist who specializes in the assessment, prevention, and treatment of child and adolescent anxiety and depression. Spence has published more than one hundred books and academic articles in her field.

Vanessa Cobham, Ph.D., holds appointments in the school of psychology at the University of Queensland and the Mater Child and Youth Mental Health Service in Brisbane, Australia.

Heidi Lyneham, Ph.D., is currently a research fellow within the department of psychology at Macquarie University and deputy director of the Centre for Emotional Health at Macquarie University in Sydney, Australia.